Scott County, Tennessee

Marriages

1854 – 1880

Byron and Barbara Sistler

JANAWAY PUBLISHING
Santa Maria, California

Scott County, Tennessee, Marriages 1854-1880

Copyright © 1988 by Byron Sistler and Barbara Sistler
All rights reserved.

Originally published, Nashville, 1988

Reprinted for
Byron Sistler and Associates, Inc.

by

Janaway Publishing, Inc.
2412 Nicklaus Dr.
Santa Maria, California 93455
(805) 925-1038
www.JanawayPublishing.com

2006, 2013

Permission to reproduce in any form
must be secured from the publisher.

ISBN: 978-1-59641-136-4

Made in the United States of America

SCOTT COUNTY, TN MARRIAGES
1854-1880

Where two dates appear on an entry, the first one is the date license was issued, the second (in parentheses) the date marriage was solemnized. If only one date, it usually means that the date of execution was the same as the date of license issuance.

Sometimes the execution of the marriage was not reported to the courthouse, and occasionally the clerk failed to note in the marriage book that the license was returned. We would usually make a notation in the entry to indicate the non-execution of a marriage if the book so stated.

The marriages are arranged alphabetically, the first half of the book by groom--the second by bride.

The records included in this book were transcribed by us directly from microfilmm of the original marriage books. Error, where it occurs, may be attributed to us, or to the clerks of the period, many of whom did an appallingly sloppy job of entering the information.

If the bride and groom were black, a B is placed at the end of the entry.

It should be remembered that this and other marriage books we have prepared are indexes, and do not include all the information to be found in the original marriage book. Such data as names of bondsmen, ministers, justices of the peace, churches, etc., are omitted. Often such information is helpful to the researcher. Consequently the serious researcher, to obtain this additional information as well as to check on the accuracy of the transcriber, should examine the original marriage record if at all possible.

Byron Sistler
Barbara Sistler

Nashville, TN
January 1988

Scott County Grooms

Abbott, Solimon to Martha E. Abbott 3-30-1880 (3-22?-1880) [S]
Acres, Daniel to Rebecca J. Griffith 11-3-1879 (11-6-1879) [S]
Acres, Dave to Luverna Phillipps 9-13-1879 (9-18-1879) [S]
Acres, J. S. to Lucinda Duncan 2-25-1876 (3-9-1876) [S]
Acres, L. J. to A. E. Hughett 5-28-1869 (5-30-1869) [S]
Acres, S. W. to Delitha Foust 11-19-1868 [S]
Alkins, Lemuel to Druesy Cook 7-14-1877 [S]
Allen, Archibald to Elizabeth M. Long 5-12-1878 [S]
Alley, Alexander S. to Rebecca Webb 9-23-1854 [S]
Anderson, David to Seney Ann Walker 10-23-1879 [S]
Anderson, George B. to Mary J. Cross 5-26-1873 8-26-1873 [S]
Anderson, James to Salley Trammell 12-23-1855 [S]
Anderson, Luke to Nancy Sharp 7-20-1877 (7-21-1877) [S]
Anderson, Timothy to Sally Gibson 7-2-1866 [S]
Anderson, W. M. to Emily Douglass 10-31-1878 [S]
Angel, James to Evaline Angel 6-4-1877 (6-10-1877) [S]
Angel, James to Narcissus Angel 7-19-1874 [S]
Angel, James jr. to Sarah E. Cross 9-8-1879 (9-18-1879) [S]
Angel, Mancil to Lucinda Angel 4-7-1876 [S]
Angel, Nimrod to Salaanay Abbott 2-15-1866 [S]
Angel, Thomas to Margery King 4-21-1872 [S]
Angel, Wm. to Nancy Meadors 8-28-1856 [S]
Asher, James to Rhody Ann Thompson 12-13-1869 12-18-1869 [S]
Atkins, Andrew J. to Eliza Ann Partin 1-18-1879 [S]
Atkins, Ewell to Sarah Cross 5-3-1877 [S]
Atkins, John C. to Parizidia Duncan 3-5-1879 [S]
Atkins, John Calvin to Burzilia Duncan 3-15-1879 (3-16-1879) [S]
Atkins, L. L. to Louezea Low 12-22-1855 12-25-1855 [S]
Atkins, L.? C. to Mary A. Burchfield 12-1-1873 12-6-1873 []
Atkins, Lacy to Emily Keeton 8-24-1875 (8-26-1875) [S]
Atkins, Lemuel to Sarah Shoopman 3-5-1855 [S]
Atkins, M. L. to Ellan Buttram 2-1-1867 [S]
Atkins, Oner to Fildiah Phellps 3-28-1879 [S]
Atkins, Ryer to Elizabeth Byrd 10-13-1865 (10-15-1865) [S]
Atkins, Thomas to Ritly Jane Low 2-9-1857 2-16-1857 [S]
Atkins, Wyatt to Rosina Chambers 1-20-1871 (1-21-1871) [S]
Ayers, James W. to Susanah Smith 12-15-1878 [S]
Babb, David to Sarah Wilhite 3-8-1878 (3-10-1878) [S]
Babb, James to Mary Lewallen 12-11-1868 [S]
Babb, S. L. to Elender Jane Wilhite 4-21-1877 (4-22-1877) [S]
Baird, William to Armeldy Trammell 6-6-1861 [S]
Baird?, Josiah to Luisa Byan 3-10-1866 3-15-1866 [S]
Baker, Calvin to Nancy Duncan 9-28-1875 (9-29-1875) [S]
Baker, R. J. to Anna B. Cordell 2-24-1877 [S]
Baker, Samuell M. to M. J. Smither 12-27-1879 (1-4-1880) [S]
Bales, John A. to Sally Price 4-8-1869 [S]
Banks, Ervin to Malinda Dagley 6-28-1875 [S]
Barnes, Thomas to Nancy J. Chitwood 5-27-1869 [S]
Barnett, Crawford to Elizabeth Hicabottum 5-14-1854 [S]
Barnett, Pennedexter to Nancy Stephens 8-4-1878 [S]
Barten, James to Martha Buttram 3-22-1879 [S]
Bartley, Milfred E. to Missouri E. Lancaster 1-15-1866 [S]
Bartly, George to Eliza Ann Prator 2-4-1867 [S]

Scott County Grooms

Bates, Josep to Myriah McPeters 11-22-1856 11-23-1856   [S]
Beacham, Henry W. to Emma Sharp 12-28-1874 (12-31-1874)   [S]
Bell, George A. to Tennessee Sandusky 11-1-1877   [S]
Bellew, Milfred to Sawannie B. Lewis 12-13-1878   [S]
Bigby, Thomas to Rhoena Sexton 1-25-1872 (2-24-1872)   [S]
Birchfield, Hesikiah to Tabbitha Crabtree 12-7-1878   [S]
Birchfield, Robert to Lucinda Jayne Tramell 12-25-1865   [S]
Bird, Burton to Mary Anderson 2-20-1856 2-24-1856   [S]
Bird, David to Mary S. Ryan 2-26-1872 (2-25?-1872)   [S]
Bird, Peter to Cumfet Cook 4-8-1857   [S]
Bird, Preecher to Mary An Byrun 9-6-1856 9-7-1856   [S]
Birge, Reddin to Lucy Ann Newport 5-24-1875   [S]
Blagben, William to Nancy Mosely 12-4-1877 (12-6-1877)   [S]
Blakely, Green A. to Elizabeth Lawson 5-1-1872   [S]
Blankenship, Caswell to Gemima Trammell 5-8-1877 (5-13-1877)   [S]
Blankenship, Daniel to Rachel Chitwood 6-8-1877 (6-10-1877)   [S]
Blankenship, Ewell B. to Lucinda Long 11-28-1877 (12-16-1877)   [S]
Blankenship, Henderson to Pernetta Jane Thompson 1-12-1876 (1-15-1876)   [S]
Blankenship, James to Emeline Trammell 8-13-1871   [S]
Blankenship, James C. to Susana Stanfill 7-2-1873   [S]
Blankinship, Wm. R. to Mary Ann Stanfll 2-11-1870 2-12-1870   [S]
Blevins, Daniel to Mary Chitwood 8-19-1870 (8-28-1870)   [S]
Blevins, Elias S. to Polly Blevins 1-6-1875   [S]
Blevins, Eligiah to Martha Smith 2-16-1876 (2-17-1876)   [S]
Blevins, John to Sureptia Terry 2-14-1870 2-15-1870   [S]
Blevins, Jonathan to Edy Sneed 4-9-1855   [S]
Blevins, Jonathin to Mary Ann Smith 4-6-1879   [S]
Blevins, Pleasant to Jane Debenport 11-19-1872 11-20-1872   [S]
Blevins, Pleasant C. to H. E. Shoopman 5-10-1870 5-22-1870   [S]
Blevins, W. C. to Charity Marcum 3-10-1878   [S]
Blevins, W. C. to Nancy Sharp 8-25-1869 (8-26-1869)   [S]
Booker, Jacob A. to Maggie Holeham 8-27-1876   [S]
Boshears, Isaac to Elizabeth Burchfield]4-10-1873   [S]
Boshears, Wm. R. H. to Huldy Boshears 9-9-1871 (9-10-1871)   [S]
Botts, James to Nancy E. Phillipps 3-17-1875 (3-21-1875)   [S]
Botts, Jerimiah to Cristeener Byrd 1-9-1878 (1-10-1878)   [S]
Botts, Jonathin to Bethany Claxton 10-2-1877   [S]
Botts, Jonathin to Nancy L. Honeycutt 9-11-1874 (9-18-1874)   [S]
Bow, William to Julia Byrd 10-14-1879 (10-18-1879)   [S]
Bowlin, Harison to Nancy Hutson 12-16-1877   [S]
Bowlin, Luke to Sarah Jane Hughett 12-11-1875   [S]
Bowline, Elihue to Thursy Ann Berge 10-11-1877   [S]
Bowling, Berry to Cristena McDonald 11-17-1864   [S]
Bowling, Berry to Pherbia Chambers 4-5-1878? (4-6-1879)   [S]
Bowling, Berry to Sarah Lewallen 1-28-1868   [S]
Bowling, Doctor to Sarah Hudson 1-26-1880   [S]
Bowling, Emanuell to Angeline Bowling 3-30-1880 (3-31-1880)   [S]
Bowling, Ewell to Mary Ann Hughett 2-27-1869 (2-28-1869)   [S]
Bowling, J. E. to Sarah A. Strunk 6-19-1875   [S]
Bowling, Thomas to Clarinday Lewallen 12-9-1854 12-10-1854   [S]
Bowling, William to Lita Keeton 3-25-1875 (4-5-1875)   [S]
Bowling, Wm. to Emely Hix 3-4-1856   [S]
Bowman, William J. to Jerushia Jane Pendler 9-3-1855   [S]
Boyatt, Abslom T. to Rebecca Jane Wattson 2-28-1879   [S]

Scott County Grooms

Boyatt, David to Sarah Winchester 4-27-1867   [S]
Boyatt, Elishia to Flemon Douglass 11-21-1871 (2-12?-1872)   [S]
Boyatt, Jordon to Mary A. Slaven 10-26-1870 (11-27-1870)   [S]
Braddy, J. L. to Mary Allen 11-18-1875   [S]
Bradley, Joshua to Kate Brantley 1-2-1880   [S]
Bradon, Granvill to Polly Smith 1-24-1866 (1-20?-1866)   [S]
Bridges, D. L. to Julian Smith 10-7-1869 (10-8-1869)   [S]
Brooks, F. M. to Mandy Phillipps 9-15-1874   [S]
Brooks, Joel L. to Lizzie Brummit 3-28-1865 (3-30-1865)   [S]
Brown, Albert to Lucinda Newport 7-19-1868   [S]
Brown, Alfred to Eliza Newport 3-19-1869   [S]
Brown, David to Milly Goad 3-1-1869 (3-2-1869)   [S]
Brown, David to Minnie Perryman 5-19-1880   [S]
Brown, George F. to Frances Williams 1-26-1880   [S]
Brown, Hamilton to Nancy Thomas 9-9-1875 (9-12-1875)   [S]
Brown, Huston to Julia Ann Marcum 2-3-1879 (2-6-1879)   [S]
Brown, John R. to Margerett Lawson 12-26-1866 12-30-1866   [S]
Brown, Lawrence to Bell Walkerson 9-25-1881   [S]
Brown, Maxwell to Myriah Phillipps 11-7-1865 (11-10-1865)   [S]
Brown, Moses to Darcus Reed 12-31-1877 (1-3-1878)   [S]
Brown, Moses to Laca Jiffer 1-6-1864 (1-5?-1864)   [S]
Brown, Tenton to Frances Hicks 9-2-1867 9-5-1867   [S]
Brown, William to Elizabeth An Johnson 12-21-1865   [S]
Brown, Winfield to Nancy C. Chambers 4-9-1872   [S]
Broyles, W. H. to Susan Gilbreath 4-4-1878   [S]
Bruce, James to Clara Birges 9-24-1870 (10-16-1870)   [S]
Bruce, James J. to Mandy L. Anderson 1-9-1876 (1-10-1876)   [S]
Bruce, John to Sousan Massingale 6-6-1875 (6-10-1875)   [S]
Bruce, L. B. to Sarah Gibson 9-9-1875   [S]
Bruce, Marion J. to Elizabeth Gibson 5-21-1878   [S]
Bruce, O. R. to Mary E. Morgan 10-31-1875 (11-20-1875)   [S]
Brunett, John to Tennessee Burton 11-13-1866   [S]
Bull, Elishia to Marry Smither 9-9-1878 (9-11-1878)   [S]
Bull, Joseph to Jane Williby 6-3-1878   [S]
Bunch, John to Patsy Low 4-1-1870 4-4-1870   [S]
Burchfield, Charley to Elizia Jane Goad 1-29-1879 (1-30-1879)   [S]
Burchfield, Robert to Lucinda Jane Tramell 12-28-1865   [S]
Burchfield, Zachariah to Rachel Honeycutt 3-12-1869 (3-14-1869)   [S]
Burk, Harmon to Polly Smith 4-1-1867 4-4-1867   [S]
Burk, Lewis to Sarah Blevins 6-11-1868   [S]
Burnett, Joseph to Lucretia Buttram 9-25-1860   [S]
Burris, Samuell to Polly Ann Marcun 12-28-1878 (12-29-1879?)   [S]
Burton, Alvin to Nancy Cenith Burton 9-21-1880   [S]
Burton, Nathan to Mary Jane Pruett 8-24-1856   [S]
Burton, William to Elizijane Trammell 6-1-1856   [S]
Buttram, Baley Jr. to Lucresy Parker 8-16-1855   [S]
Buttram, C. C. to Annalisa Newport 2-24-1875 (2-25-1875)   [S]
Buttram, Joel to Arbanna Ellis 12-26-1866 12-27-1866   [S]
Buttram, Jordian to Orbanna Buttram 7-29-1854   [S]
Buttram, Wesley to Martha King 10-25-1870 (1-22-1871)   [S]
Buttram, William to Silvia Strunk 2-14-1872   [S]
Byrd, Alfred to Martha Jane Brahears 4-11-1870   [S]
Byrd, Jerry to Louisa Smith 8-6-1854   [S]
Byrd, John to Emily (Miss) Terry 3-19-1878 (3-21-1878)   [S]

Scott County Grooms

Byrd, John to Parizidia Delk 3-8-1855   [S]
Byrd, Melton A. to Nancy Chitwood 6-24-1871 (7-1-1871)   [S]
Byrd, O. P. to Hannah Sharp 11-18-1868 (11-22-1868)   [S]
Byrd, Peter to Salina Huckoby 3-25-1880 (3-28-1880)   [S]
Byrd, Thomas to Maria Delk 2-4-1856   [S]
Byrd, William to Mary Huttson 11-7-1870 (11-10-1870)   [S]
Byrd, William R. to Martha J. Jeffers 10-15-1879 (10-16-1879)   [S]
Byrd, Zachariah to Snitha Marcum 4-17-1874   [S]
Callist, Ruford to Ellie V. Davis 12-10-1878   [S]
Camble, Green B. to Elizabeth Goodin 4-23-1860   [S]
Cameron?, Lewis to Jane McKinley 10-19-1878 (10-20-1878)   [S]
Canada, William J. to Susana J. Duncan 10-14-1859 (10-16-1859)   [S]
Canor, John to Sarah Casey 11-29-1875 (11-30-1875)   [S]
Caroll, Alexander to Susana Massingale 9-25-1872 9-29-1872   [S]
Caroll, Huston to Angeline Mason 7-30-1869   [S]
Caroll, William to Nancy Bowling 4-13-1861 (4-14-1861)   [S]
Carrol, William to Juannah Canada 1-5-1865   [S]
Carroll, Willy to Almiriah McDonald 1-10-1870   [S]
Carson, George to Manda J. Hail 3-18-1880 (3-21-1880)   [S]
Carson, Jackson to Nancy J. Terry 10-4-1871   [S]
Carson, John jr. to Lucy A. Chitwood 1-3-1876 (1-6-1876)   [S]
Carson, John, Jr. to Lucinda Terry 9-25-1873   [S]
Carson, Samuel to Sarah Willhite 10-28-1867 (10-31-1867)   [S]
Carson, Samul to Emily Reed 11-15-1871 (11-16-1871)   [S]
Carson, Wm. H. to Parley Pemberton 5-14-1875   [S]
Cecil, Baty to Polly Buttram 11-4-1874 (11-6-1874)   [S]
Cecil, George W. to Olly David 8-9-1879 (8-21-1879)   [S]
Cecil, Isaac to Olly Tapley 12-18-1859   [S]
Cecil, James T.? to Phoeba Phillipps 1-10-1872 (1-11-1872)   [S]
Cecil, Josep to Susan Sandusky 9-20-1865   [S]
Cecil, Nelson to Manervia S.? Massingale 9-21-1867 9-22-1867   [S]
Cecil, Reuben to Lovina Marcum 9-26-1874 (9-27-1874)   [S]
Cecil, William R. to loucinda Thomas 8-4-1873 8-17-1873   [S]
Cellars, G. W. to Artinisey Strunk 10-29-1875   [S]
Cellers, J. M. to Jenetta Silars 8-30-1878   [S]
Chamber, Calvin to Martha A. Huett 10-7-1872 10-8-1872   [S]
Chambers, Calvin to Lucretia A. Buttram 10-19-1876   [S]
Chambers, Calvin to Mary Martha Sharp 6-4-1870 6-5-1870   [S]
Chambers, Calvin to Sarah Pitman 1-26-1876 (1-27-1876)   [S]
Chambers, Daniel to Polly West 12-13-1874   [S]
Chambers, Elihue to Angeline Blakely 1-18-1876 (1-19-1876)   [S]
Chambers, Ewell to Pherby Birge 8-29-1872   [S]
Chambers, Francis Marion to Lucinda Lay 9-13-1864 (9-15-1864)   [S]
Chambers, George W. to Nancy Cross 3-16-1867   [S]
Chambers, Granville C. to Rebecca Cross 4-23-1865 (4-27-1865)   [S]
Chambers, Jerrymiah to Rebecca Willhite 2-4-1855 2-27-1855   [S]
Chambers, John to Creasanor Anderson 12-24-1855 12-25-1855   [S]
Chambers, Pleasant to Jane Phillipps 12-20-1877 (12-23-1877)   [S]
Chambers, Riley to Mary Byrd 2-17-1867   [S]
Chambers, S. L. to Helen Sharp 3-13-1869 (3-14-1869)   [S]
Chambers, T. M. jr. to Rachel D. Lay 1-20-1875 (1-21-1875)   [S]
Chambers, Thomas to Lucinda Batts 1-14-1879 (1-19-1879)   [S]
Chambers, Thomas to Lucinda Dowirs? 7-28-1879   [S]
Chambers, Thomas to Sarah Lay 4-29-1863   [S]

Scott County Grooms

Chambers, W. R. to Nancy Lawson 1-13-1866 (1-14-1866)   [S]
Chambers, W. S. to Mary Provine 10-13-1869   [S]
Chambers, William to Mary J. Brown 7-1-1878 (7-4-1878)   [S]
Chambers, Winfield S. to Rebecca Stanley 12-16-1879   [S]
Chandler, William F. to Burnetta J. Chambers 5-10-1871 (5-11-1871)   [S]
Chaney, Nicholas T. to Lucinda Lewallen 12-4-1856 12-9-1856   [S]
Childers, Holbert to Mary Parry 6-26-1866   [S]
Childers, James to Rebecca Anderson 5-1-1879   [S]
Childers, William to Polly Taylor 8-12-1880   [S]
Chitwood, A. D. to Polly Chitwood 9-28-1869 (10-1-1869)   [S]
Chitwood, Andrew to Elizabeth (Miss) Duncan 10-8-1878 (10-10-1878)   [S]
Chitwood, Calvin to Sarah Sego 10-10-1861   [S]
Chitwood, David to Nancy Cambell 4-2-1860 (4-12-1860)   [S]
Chitwood, Ewell to Phoeba Emery 9-20-1868   [S]
Chitwood, F. M. to Emily Chitwood 5-13-1876 (5-18-1876)   [S]
Chitwood, G. W. to Mary Jane Blevins 8-24-1869 (8-26-1869)   [S]
Chitwood, Harvy to Valeyor? Tramell 2-25-1874 (3-16-1874)   [S]
Chitwood, James G. to Rebecca Reed 2-16-1865   [S]
Chitwood, James L. to Martha Jane Thompson 2-28-1878   [S]
Chitwood, Joel C. to Mary Jane Trammell 3-22-1876 (3-23-1876)   [S]
Chitwood, L. D. to Sarah Chitwood 8-20-1871   [S]
Chitwood, Linsay to Melda (Miss) Baker 10-18-1877   [S]
Chitwood, Richard to Lorie Chitwood 5-17-1876 (5-18-1876)   [S]
Chitwood, Sterling to Lenory Stephens 10-3-1876 (10-5-1876)   [S]
Chitwood, William to Nancy Taylor 2-26-1879 (2-20?-1879)   [S]
Christia, Albert to Shillotty Cornillas 7-18-1875   [S]
Christian, Thomas to Thursy Ann Byrd 2-1-1872   [S]
Clark, Jerry to Sarah Whiting 12-18-1875   [S]
Claxton, George to Louisa Honeycutt 1-2-1878 (1-3-1878)   [S]
Claxton, James to Elizabeth Atkins 6-5-1874 (6-7-1874)   [S]
Claxton, Wm. to Sarah Abbit 9-5-1877 (12-7-1877)   [S]
Clours, J. N. to Martha Gosnel 8-13-1875 (8-16-1875)   [S]
Coffey, Harden to Jane Watters 7-31-1866   [S]
Coffey, James S. to Melvina _____ 11-16-1878   [S]
Coffey, John to Elizabeth Strunk 3-16-1861 (3-17-1861)   [S]
Coffey, Lewis to Isabella Cooper 1-3-1879 (1-30-1879)   [S]
Collins, Charles to Margett A. Reed 12-29-1875   [S]
Conatser, Reuben to Sarah E. Lackey 11-14-1873 11-15-1873   [S]
Conner, David O. to Ibb. McDowell 8-19-1879 (8-29-1879)   [S]
Cooper, E. W. to Elizabeth Hutson 1-28-1869   [S]
Cooper, Eli to Gemmina J. Taylor 12-11-1871   [S]
Cooper, Henry to Elizabeth Stephens 12-12-1855 1-12-1855?   [S]
Cooper, J. F. to R. M. Taylor 12-11-1871   [S]
Cooper, James to Elizabeth Price 2-25-1860 (4-19-1860)   [S]
Cooper, John to Elizabeth Wilson 4-7-1876 (4-9-1876)   [S]
Cooper, Linsay to Elizabeth Stephens 3-11-1861   [S]
Cooper, Thomas to Esther Griffeth 5-1-1861   [S]
Cooper, Washington to Tellithia Can Atkins 8-6-1868   [S]
Cordell, A. J. to Sarah E. Moser 2-1-1875   [S]
Cordell, David B. to Gracie Rose 8-31-1856   [S]
Cordell, James to Olive Cox 8-27-1857   [S]
Cordell, John M. to China W. Cotton 12-25-1860 (1-24-1861)   [S]
Cordell, Joseph M. to Nancy E. S. Strunk 12-6-1866   [S]
Cordell, W. H. to Lucy Strunk 3-18-1861   [S]

Scott County Grooms

Cordell, William to Mary L. Creekmore 2-20-1856 2-21-1856   [S]
Cordell, William J. to Armelia Davis 2-27-1875   [S]
Cordell, Wm. to Jeny Phillipps 12-29-1869 1-2-1870   [S]
Cornelas, Henry to Elizabeth Hatfield 8-24-1856   [S]
Cornelias, Elishia to Rebecca Mahaly 12-31-1854   [S]
Costella, Micheal to Reminy Hart 6-2-1876   [S]
Cotton, F. W. to Melvina Phillipps 5-17-1869   [S]
Cotton, Tasmon W. to Mary Ann Carson 9-24-1867 9-26-1867   [S]
Cowen, William to Arreny Flynn 10-27-1876   [S]
Cox, James to Delphia Fredrick 1-23-1860   [S]
Cox, John to Salina Hix 8-27-1867 9-3-1867   [S]
Cox, John W. to Parezidia Lay 3-11-1873   [S]
Cox, W. H. to Elizabeth Bowling 10-12-1864   [S]
Crabtree, Abslom to Jane Cooper 5-22-1877   [S]
Crabtree, James to Mary E. Stanly 3-23-1875 (3-24-1875)   [S]
Crabtree, John to Nancy Marcum 5-12-1875 (5-13-1875)   [S]
Crabtree, Richard to Emma Shelton 8-28-1878 (8-29-1878)   [S]
Crabtree, Russle to Jane Gregory 9-15-1877   [S]
Crabtree, William to Parazidia Standly 3-12-1868   [S]
Crabtree, William to Sarah Gentry 9-5-1860   [S]
Crabtree, William A. to Melvina Trammell 10-24-1874 (10-25-1874)   [S]
Craft, G. W. to Emmarine Slaven 12-28-1871   [S]
Craig, Isaac K. to Marth Chitwood 1-16-1861   [S]
Creekmore, Dauze H. to Nella Brown 2-14-1878 (2-15-1878)   [S]
Creekmore, Even to Nancy Jane Smith 1-15-1857   [S]
Creekmore, Francis A. to Permelia Cain 1-7-1858   [S]
Creekmore, G. B. to Elizabeth Chitwood 7-4-1870 7-17-1870   [S]
Creekmore, Henry to Virginia E. Elson 9-18-1872 9-29-1872   [S]
Creekmore, J. C. to Mary Taylor 7-18-1872 9-29-1872   [S]
Creekmore, Richard to Rhoda Grant 2-17-1877   [S]
Creekmore, Thomas B. to Emily Neal 12-5-1876   [S]
Creyson, Augusta? to Elizabeth Hould 3-26-1875 (3-28-1875)   [S]
Croly, Lewis to E. J. Chambers 4-14-1875 (4-15-1875)   [S]
Cronin, Daniel to Elizabeth Smith 5-4-1875   [S]
Cross, A. J. to Salley Patterson 1-2-1856 1-3-1856   [S]
Cross, Abslom to Florina Jeffers 9-1-1879   [S]
Cross, Alfred to Samantha J. Atkins 1-13-1880 (1-17-1880)   [S]
Cross, E. M. to Lucinda Grant 2-21-1880   [S]
Cross, Emanuel to Ester Cooper 4-1-1869 (4-4-1869)   [S]
Cross, Emanuel to Mandy Lay 10-24-1868 (10-25-1868)   [S]
Cross, Ewell to Martha Williams 1-12-1874   [S]
Cross, H. W. to Elizabeth Griffith 10-16-1871   [S]
Cross, Hensey T.? to Nancy Rookard 3-6-1876 (3-12-1876)   [S]
Cross, Jacob L. to Rebecca Chambers 9-29-1859   [S]
Cross, Jacob Q.? to Myriah J. Low 1-4-1871 (1-19-1871)   [S]
Cross, Joseph to Marleny Atkins 11-8-1873 11-20-1873   [S]
Cross, Rufus to Elizabeth Atkins 3-5-1878 (3-7-1878)   [S]
Cross, Thomas to Elizabeth Phillipps 2-14-1878 (2-21-1878)   [S]
Cross, William to E. A. Ross 7-9-1863   [S]
Cross, William H. to Mary Lay 5-10-1879 (5-25-1879)   [S]
Cross, William L. to Kiziah Shoopman 12-5-1866   [S]
Crumley, Allen W. to Rhoda Scott 6-27-1876   [S]
Cumins, J. S. to Martha E. Davenport 10-19-1878   [S]
Cummins, J. S. to Martha Davenport 10-19-1878   [S]

Scott County Grooms

Dagley, Russle to Emely Stanley 12-27-1860 [S]
Daughty, James to M. Drucilla Childers 4-27-1879 [S]
Daughty, Jesse to Tabbitha Trammell 11-1-1855 [S]
Daughty, John to Martha West 8-19-1878 (8-20-1878) [S]
Daughty, Pleasant to Mary Garrett 8-2-1880 (8-5-1880) [S]
Davenport, G. B. to Julia Ann Ryan 2-3-1879 [S]
Davenport, J. A. to Mahala Ball 10-1-1877 (10-7-1877) [S]
Davenport, James G. to Helen Strunk 1-9-1869 (1-7?-1869) [S]
David, Jacob to Rachel L. Phillipps 1-15-1876 (1-20-1876) [S]
Davidson, Jacob to Elizabeth Newport 3-14-1878 [S]
Davidson, Samuel to Elizabeth Smither 3-31-1856 4-2-1856 [S]
Davis, Charles W. to Dusa O. Sheppard 4-20-1880 (4-18?-1880) [S]
Davis, James to Matilda Smith 4-6-1856 [S]
Davis, Joseph to Elizabeth Young 11-17-1865 (12-5-1865) [S]
Davis, Marion to Jane Webb 1-28-1879 [S]
Davis, Phillipp to Delitha Lean Hatfield 2-18-1869 [S]
Davis, R. S. to Mary Duncan 8-8-1874 (8-9-1874) [S]
Davis, Stephen E. to Mary Jane Williams 1-11-1868 [S]
Davis, W. H. to Rachel Thompson 4-29-1869 (5-2-1869) [S]
Davis, W. L. to Manda Phillipps 4-3-1869 (4-4-1869) [S]
Davis, Wilson to Lucinda Chitwood 5-29-1856 [S]
Dawn, Henry C. to Lydia S. Duncan 11-30-1870 (12-1-1870) [S]
Dean, A. C. to Mandy Keeton 11-11-1879 (11-6?-1879) [S]
Debenport, F. M. to Relda Pambly 6-10-1871 (6-28-1871) [S]
Deboys, Thomas to Pherbia Buttram 12-30-1877 [S]
Debty, William L. to Jane Smith 7-6-1879 (7-7-1879) [S]
Debty, William L. to Peggy Ann Phillipp 11-29-1878 (not executed) [S]
Decker, John M. to Annie Bell 5-10-1876 (5-12-1876) [S]
Denny, Ruben M. to Ellen (Miss) Fair 11-19-1876 [S]
Dick, G. P. to Mary Jane Thompson 5-3-1880 (5-13-1880) [S]
Dick, J. Q.? to Ma A. Craig 2-16-1874 (2-17-1874) [S]
Dick, James to Almirah Burk 2-28-1871 [S]
Diden, John to Martha Young 9-11-1872 9-12-1872 [S]
Dobbs, Fleoman to Relda Koger 9-8-1878 [S]
Dobbs, Henderson to Eliza B. Sharp 12-15-1878 [S]
Domini, Vilantia to Sarah Roberson 6-5-1879 (6-6-1879) B [S]
Douglass, Ewell to M. E. Cordell 2-9-1879 [S]
Drawn, James to Clorie A. Griffith 3-29-1877 (4-1-1877) [S]
Duncan, Champion to Louisa Emeline Jane Duncan 2-2-1860 [S]
Duncan, David to Armelda Chitwood 6-3-1869 (7-25-1869) [S]
Duncan, E. R. to Elizabeth Scott 7-7-1857 7-9-1856 [S]
Duncan, Emanuel to Jane Cecil 3-1-1869 (3-4-1869) [S]
Duncan, F. A. to Sarah Strunk 1-7-1869 [S]
Duncan, Gideon to Lurania Rutha Risden 12-21-1859 (12-22-1859) [S]
Duncan, Granvill C. to Helen m. Sharp 11-8-1873 10-8-1873? [S]
Duncan, Henry to Polly Harness 1-5-1860 (1-6-1860) [S]
Duncan, J. J. to Maria Sintha Cross 8-17-1854 [S]
Duncan, J. S. to Rosa Jane Buttram 2-24-1870 3-3-1870 [S]
Duncan, Joel to Martha Ann Ross 5-1-1880 (5-2-1880) [S]
Duncan, Joshua to Ester R. Strunk 4-16-1876 (4-21-1876) [S]
Duncan, Joshua to Martha Thomas 1-6-1871 (1-13-1871) [S]
Duncan, Joshua to Sarah Trammell 10-5-1877 [S]
Duncan, Marion to Jane Foster 1-14-1868 (1-16-1868) [S]
Duncan, Micheal to Margerett Harness 6-16-1880 (6-26-1880) [S]

Scott County Grooms

Duncan, Newton to Martha A. Jeffers 10-6-1870   [S]
Duncan, Oliver to Rutha Duncan 3-11-1856 (3-13-1856)   [S]
Duncan, Rhodes to Elizabeth E. Cordell 11-14-1878   [S]
Duncan, W. M. to Sarah Mason 12-6-1873 (12-7-1873)   [S]
Dunn, P. B. to M. A. Toole 4-24-1876 (4-25-1876)   [S]
Durm, S. B. to Betty Ann Ross 6-29-1878   [S]
Dyer, Joel to Rebecca Anne Sexton 3-3-1880 (3-4-1880)   [S]
Eadds, Jno. to Nancy Webb 1-20-1871 (1-21-1871)   [S]
Eads, George to Nancy J. Marcun 6-15-1871   [S]
Edward, Sanders L. to Elisa Roberson 2-28-1877   [S]
Elam, James W. to Susan Mulnes 1-1-1867   [S]
Elder, Jacob to Mattie Colens 9-20-1880   [S]
Eliott, James G. to Jane Bridges 9-1-1873 9-4-1873   [S]
Elliott, James Mattison to Sarah Ellis 11-15-1860 (11-18-1860)   [S]
Ellis, Andrew J. to Rosey J. Parker 12-17-1879 (12-18-1879)   [S]
Ellis, Calaway to Huldy Buttram 3-22-1875 (3-28-1875)   [S]
Ellis, Edward to Clerinda Reed 12-20-1871   [S]
Ellis, Edward to Phenly Silcox 7-13-1867   []
Ellis, Eward to Martha Silcox 10-19-1875 (10-31-1875)   [S]
Ellis, Marion to Martha Jane Ellis 8-13-1866   [S]
Ellis, Martin to Thursy Jane Parker 11-7-1868 (11-8-1868)   [S]
Ellis, Trumon to Martha A. Marcum 4-23-1874 (4-26-1874)   [S]
Ellis, William to Sarah Batts 1-27-1876 (1-17?-1876)   [S]
Ellis, William R. to Nancy Phillipp 10-10-1876 (10-12-1876)   [S]
Elswick, James L. to Sarah Ann Chitwood 2-27-1867 2-28-1867   [S]
Epperson, John to Nancy Byrd 4-24-1870   [S]
Ervin, Calvin to Caroline Kirby 12-14-1877 (12-16-1877)   [S]
Evins, Louis C. to Mary Wilouby 11-21-1879 (11-22-1879)   [S]
Evins, Samuell to Sarah Blevins 1-25-1876 (1-27-1876)   [S]
Faron, Levi to Nancy Adkerson 4-6-1865   [S]
Faron, Levy to Nancy E. Adkerson 4-6-1865   [S]
Filser, Hiram to Rebecca Thompson 7-14-1876 (7-27-1876)   [S]
Foster, Charles to Lurany Terry 8-12-1875 (8-15-1875)   [S]
Foster, Ervin to Elvis Slavin 10-18-1864   [S]
Foster, Isaac to Jane Troxwell 1-15-1870   [S]
Foster, Isaac to Relda Forbis 9-16-1880   [S]
Foster, Jacob to Jane A. Lay 8-5-1877   [S]
Foster, James to Lucy Ellis 2-20-1869 (2-24-1869)   [S]
Foster, James G. to Matilda Ramsey 3-5-1860 (3-6-1860)   [S]
Foster, John to Clarisa Ellis 4-1-1868 (4-2-1868)   [S]
Foster, John to Emeline Phillipp 9-27-1878 (10-3-1878)   [S]
Foster, Morris to Jane Reliford 3-27-1880 (3-28-1880)   [S]
Freels, Squire to Rachel Lay 12-27-1878 (12-22?-1878)   [S]
Freeman, J. R. to Molly M. C. Welch 11-7-1875 (11-8-1875)   [S]
Frosts, R. M. to Marica Strunk 8-1-1874   [S]
Gadson, Isaac to Almeda Coal 3-14-1875   [S]
Gant, Thomas to Sarah Strunk 3-22-1876 (3-23-1876)   [S]
Garlen, G. C. to Milly Johnson 3-15-1869   [S]
Gaston, William to Susan E. Burgan 8-3-1867   [S]
Gauly, Pat to Sarah Grining 6-8-1876   [S]
Gentry, Calvin to Luverna Marcum 6-5-1862   [S]
Gibson, Alfred to Sarah Bowlen 7-29-1879 (7-30-1879)   [S]
Gibson, Isaac to Lotty Hammons 3-16-1866   [S]
Gibson, James to Malinda Taylor 9-1-1870   [S]

Gibson, James E. to Kiziah Acres 7-4-1870 7-21-1870 [S]
Gibson, Jessie to America Ingrum 11-30-1875 [S]
Gibson, Jessie to Sarah Wootson 6-15-1872 6-19-1872 [S]
Gibson, Johnson to Partely Anderson 11-10-1877 (11-11-1877) [S]
Gibson, Wm. R. to Sarah Ann Roberson 3-11-1872 [S]
Gilbreth, J. L. to A.R. Meadors 12-7-1857 (1-7-1857?) [S]
Gillis, John to Katie Harwick 4-6-1875 [S]
Gillis, John J. to Katie Harwich 4-6-1875 [S]
Glover, William to Nancy C. Mounts 1-14-1878 [S]
Goad, James to Purdyan Young 3-31-1855 [S]
Goad, John to Elizabeth Smither 6-4-1878 (6-6-1878) [S]
Goad, L. B. to Martha J. Todd 11-21-1873 [S]
Goad, Wm. to Hatty Griffith 2-12-1857 [S]
Goins, Melton to Sarah J. Smith 2-25-1865 2-26-1865 [S]
Golden, Demsey to Emeline Saloan? 7-7-1876 [S]
Gonins?, Melton to Sarah Jane Smith 2-6-1865 [S]
Good, Kilonnon? F. to Mattie Orlena Laxton 1-19-1875 (1-21-1875) [S]
Goodin, Martin to Layer? Goodin 8-8-1879 [S]
Goodman, Alexander to Louisa? Atkins 8-4-1873 8-7-1873 [S]
Goodman, Andrew to Evy Jane Massingale 9-18-1877 (9-20-1877) [S]
Goodman, Jesse to Julian Masongale 4-3-1863 (4-5-1865?) [S]
Goodwin, Jno. to Jane Low 1-30-1859 [S]
Gosalin, Freelin to Jane Alley 11-4-1854 11-5-1854 [S]
Grant, James to Sarah A. Neal 9-5-1880 (7?-15-1880) [S]
Gregory, D. A. to Margarett E. Wallen 8-28-1872 [S]
Gregory, Eli to Martha Hurtt 4-13-1879 [S]
Gregory, William H. to Mary M. Roberts 10-22-1879 (10-23-1879) [S]
Grider, G. W. to Pheba Massingale 7-23-1869 (7-31-1869) [S]
Griffeth, Hamilton to Adiline Lawson 9-30-1868 (10-18-1868) [S]
Griffith, Alexander to Sarah E. Sexton 11-18-1876 (11-19-1876) [S]
Griffith, Allen to Rebecca Loyd 9-30-1862 [S]
Griffith, Andrew to Lucinda Newport 7-3-1865 (7-6-1865) [S]
Griffith, Andrew to Malinda Goad 3-30-1857 4-2-1857 [S]
Griffith, Daniel to Rosetta Pemberton 12-16-1873 (12-18-1873) [S]
Griffith, Elswick to Margerett Phillipps 11-11-1879 (11-13-1879) [S]
Griffith, Ivery F. to Miriah Goswell 12-15-1876 (12-17-1876) [S]
Griffith, James to Mary Peak 8-15-1878 [S]
Griffith, James to Sarah Ann Rich 6-2-1871 (6-3-1871) [S]
Griffith, Joel to Jane Griffith 1-14-1878 (1-16-1878) [S]
Griffith, John to Elizabeth Goad 11-16-1870 (11-18-1870) [S]
Griffith, Josep to Sarah Newport 11-23-1860 [S]
Griffith, Reuben to Rozana Young 4-4-1874 (4-9-1874) [S]
Griffith, Richard to Emily Newport 6-20-1874 (6-25-1874) [S]
Griffith, William to Catharine Sexton 4-9-1866 [S]
Griffith, William to Catharine Sexton 4-9-1866 12-9-1866 [S]
Griffith, Wright to Rebecca Newport 11-18-1879 (11-21-1879) [S]
Grigory, W. H. to Artymsy Bell 5-27-1878 (5-21?-1878) [S]
Guin, Joseph to Creesy Phillipps 9-6-1879 (9-7-1879) [S]
Hacker, William to Mary Curtis 11-17-1859 [S]
Haden, Perry to Lizzie Jasper 8-19-1880 [S]
Hale, Thomas to Mary J. Goodan 7-26-1879 (7-28-1879) [S]
Hall, John M. to Sarah Thompson 9-9-1876 (9-10-1876) [S]
Halmon, John to Jane Bowlin 8-26-1875 (8-29-1875) [S]
Hamblin, Tyrell to Sarah Chambers 10-14-1861 (10-15-1861) [S]

Scott County Grooms

Hamby, Frank to Mary Keeth 1-19-1860   [S]
Hamby, James C. to Sarah Begly 7-27-1874 (8-6-1874)   [S]
Hamby, John to Emily Sexton 3-29-1875 (4-18-1875)   [S]
Hamby, William to Rhody A. Sexton 10-8-1871   [S]
Hamby, William H. to Sarah Lay 12-16-1871   [S]
Hammock, D. H. to Elizabeth Thompson 9-15-1879   [S]
Hammock, Rufus Asberry to Nancy Thompson 12-27-1879 (1-1-1880)   [S]
Hammon, Jacob to Rosa Buttram 10-30-1856   [S]
Hamons, Minza to Anna Taylor 7-4-1858   [S]
Harden, Isaac to Mary Sweet 6-13-1868   [S]
Hardick, A. J. to Litha Lovall 6-9-1867   [S]
Hardwick, Robert to Easter Balloo 2-20-1861   [S]
Hardy, Frank to Sarah J. Goodman 5-30-1876 (5-3?-1876)   [S]
Harmon, James to Eliza J. Tengel? 12-27-1868   [S]
Harmon, Kindricke to Ellen Smith 9-25-1866 1-6-1867   [S]
Harness, Jerimiah to Elmiriah Brown 2-1-1873 2-2-1873   [S]
Harness, Jerimiah to Leaner Sexton 1-8-1878 (1-24-1878)   [S]
Harness, John to Elizabeth Harness 1-5-1860 (2-11-1860)   [S]
Harness, John to Surrelda Harness 8-13-1873   [S]
Harness, John R. to Mary Angeline Foster 3-24-1872   [S]
Harness, Newton to Sarah Bowlin 10-4-1875 (10-13-1875)   [S]
Harness, Samuell to Susanah Bowling 1-7-1879 (1-9-1879)   [S]
Harness, Thomas W. to Nancy Jane Brown 10-11-1865 (10-12-1865)   [S]
Harness, William to Elvina Brown 7-23-1868   [S]
Harness, William R. to Gincy Harness 8-7-1872 8-8-1872   [S]
Harrison, Geo. W. to Bertha F. Cassifang 9-2-1875 (9-5-1875)   [S]
Hatfield, Calvin to Angeline Bowling 11-11-1871   [S]
Hatfield, Calvin to Mary Reatherford 4-30-1880 (4-4?-1880)   [S]
Hatfield, David to Esther Phillips 7-8-1865   [S]
Hatfield, David to Esther Phillips 7-8-1865   [S]
Hatfield, David to Kizah Phillips 7-8-1865   [S]
Hatfield, Hansford to Eliza Elliott 4-8-1854 4-9-1854   [S]
Hatfield, J. F. to Manerva Gibson 5-6-1861 (5-12-1861)   [S]
Hatfield, J. G. to Susanah (Miss) Kidd 12-18-1877 (12-24-1877)   [S]
Hatfield, James to Pricy Riethley 12-22-1875 (12-23-1875)   [S]
Hatfield, Joseph to Agny Bruce 4-18-1877   [S]
Hatfield, Stephen to R. I. Smith 2-11-1854 2-12-1854   [S]
Hatfield, W. A. to Burnettia Gibson 1-6-1866 (1-17-1866)   [S]
Hatmaker, John to Arbanna Keeton 1-13-1880   [S]
Hays, Anderson to Susanah Stephens 2-13-1875 (2-14-1875)   [S]
Hays, Joel R. to M. E. Robinson 8-16-1877   [S]
Hays, John to Lurania Ryan 10-16-1866   [S]
Hays, Thomas to Rachel M. Neal 3-9-1879   [S]
Hays, Thomas (or James) to Alley Ryan 7-3-1856   [S]
Heath, James to Kizzia Ross 5-13-1878   [S]
Hembree, Alvis to Matilda Goodman 1-5-1879 (3-20-1879)   [S]
Hembree, Ezekiel to Barzilia Bunch ?-15-1865 (3-19-1865)   [S]
Hembree, Hugh to Nancy Jane Hughett 11-17-1855 11-19-1855   [S]
Hembree, J. H. to Rebecca J. Low 4-1-1874 (4-9-1874)   [S]
Hembree, William O. to Emely Shoopman 7-23-1859 (7-24-1859)   [S]
Hendree, Oliver to Jane Phillipps 8-19-1880   [S]
Hendrick, Jacob to Lisey Brummett 12-24-1875 (12-25-1875)   [S]
Henry, John C. to Rebecca Griffith 9-7-1868 (9-10-1868)   [S]
Hensey, Allen to Tilda Nelson 5-10-1876   [S]

Scott County Grooms

Hensly, Narmis to Margerett Powers 9-25-1880   [S]
Hicks, Anderson to Emely Brown 7-12-1869 (7-13-1869)   [S]
Hicks, Jessie to Elizabeth Sweet 6-21-1876 (6-29-1876)   [S]
Hicks, Thomas to Nancy Shelton 4-2-1868   [S]
Hicks, Thomas to Nancy Shelton 4-5-1869   [S]
Highton, G. B. to harriett Soloman 10-13-1880   [S]
Hill, Berry to Louisa Cross 8-23-1877 (8-26-1877)   [S]
Hill, Ely to (bride omitted) 9-11-1859   [S]
Hill, Henry to Sarah Tackett 4-18-1860 (4-19-1860)   [S]
Hill, Isaac to Elizia Jane Coill 12-2-1855   [S]
Hill, Isaac to Mary E. Kidd 6-11-1877 (6-13-1877)   [S]
Hill, James H. to Delphia S. Strunk 10-15-1859   [S]
Hill, Joab to Polley Chitwood 7-23-1865 (7-25-1865)   [S]
Hill, Richard to Elizabeth Stidheam 4-10-1877 (4-22-1877)   [S]
Hinson, John to Nancy Ann Moses 8-28-1868   [S]
Hix, Marion to Malinda Penington 3-6-1865 (3-10-1865)   [S]
Holt, Joel to Mary L. Roberts 2-13-1879   [S]
Honeycutt, Bryant to Sureptia Bridges 10-3-1864   [S]
Honeycutt, Edward to Mary J. Marcum 2-16-1873   [S]
Honeycutt, Edward to Mary J. Marcum 2-16-1873 2-26-1873   [S]
Honeycutt, Jarrett to Mary Jane Claxton 3-9-1878 (3-10-1878)   [S]
Honeycutt, John to Catharine Hatfield 10-3-1859 (10-6-1859)   [S]
Honeycutt, Thomas to Elizabeth Bridges 2-21-1860   [S]
Honeycutt, Uriah to Nancy Bridges 10-10-1861   [S]
Honeycutt, William to Frances Rosser 12-23-1865 (12-24-1865)   [S]
Hoss, John to Mary A. Sharp 10-3-1874 (10-4-1874)   [S]
Huckobey, Pressly to Rittie A. Cross 5-29-1878 (5-30-1878)   [S]
Huff, Hiram to Polly Keath 3-13-1877   [S]
Hugett, Calvin to Rebecca E. Elliott 1-2-1869 (1-3-1869)   [S]
Hughett, James to Polly Phillipps 3-2-1875   [S]
Hughett, Jasper to Vicy (Miss) Robbins 1-16-1877 (1-18-1877)   [S]
Hughett, John F. to Mandy Robbins 3-6-1871 (3-23-1871)   [S]
Hughett, Robin to Pollyan Brown 6-14-1857   [S]
Hughett, W. H. to Lakey Jayne Pennington 11-21-1864   [S]
Hull, N. R. to Mary Massingale 10-2-1876 (10-5-1876)   [S]
Human, E. A. to Franky Griffith 6-8-1873   [S]
Human, Wm. H. to Frances Low 10-3-1871   [S]
Hunly, James to Peggy Spradling 1-22-1855   [S]
Hurtt, Moses F. to Ellen Atkins 12-20-1870 (12-22-1870)   [S]
Hurtt, Ruben to Oliff Sexton 1-17-1876 (1-20-1876)   [S]
Huse, G. W. to Mary Solomon 8-28-1877   [S]
Hutson, Carter to Lovina Cruse 10-7-1874 (10-5?-1874)   [S]
Hutson, William to Elizabeth Byrd 3-26-1872   [S]
Inman, Joseph to Sarah E. Helton 12-10-1876 (12-6?-1876)   [S]
Jackson, J. W. to Nancy Ann Harrison 10-9-1866 3-9-1866?   [S]
James, Dillard to Jennie Ervin 11-11-1874   B [S]
Jasper, W. R. Riley to Mary C. Surber 3-28-1879   [S]
Jeffers, C. R. to Delily Harness 8-18-1877 (8-14?-1877)   [S]
Jeffers, Champion to Malinda York 5-17-1866   [S]
Jeffers, Claborn to Melvinia Philipps 6-11-1872 6-20-1872   [S]
Jeffers, Claborn to Nancy Chambers 5-1-1867 5-2-1867   [S]
Jeffers, Daniel to Sarah Hembree 12-24-1860 (12-27-1860)   [S]
Jeffers, David to Phoeba J. Yancy 1-27-1871 (2-2-1871)   [S]
Jeffers, Emsley to Elmiriah Chambers 3-31-1855 4-5-1855   [S]

Scott County Grooms

Jeffers, Emsley to Margerett Chambers 10-18-1855   [S]
Jeffers, Emsley to Sarah Newport 1-5-1875 (1-7-1875)   [S]
Jeffers, Franklin to Sarah Chambers 1-7-1879 (1-10-1879)   [S]
Jeffers, Huston to Elizabeth Yancy 4-30-1872   [S]
Jeffers, Isaac to Nancy Clay Thompson 5-18-1874   [S]
Jeffers, Isaac sr. to Pernetta Phillipps 3-7-1874   [S]
Jeffers, James to Lucrecia Harriess 2-18-1876 (2-20-1876)   [S]
Jeffers, James to Omy Boshears 6-11-1870 6-12-1870   [S]
Jeffers, Julen S. to Delila Ownes 9-2-1880 (9-23-1880)   [S]
Jeffers, Julin to Lucinda Bowlin 8-29-1878   [S]
Jeffers, Marion to Mary Jane Reynals 3-21-1878   [S]
Jeffers, Oliver to Lucinda York 6-17-1867   [S]
Jeffers, Pleasan to Charlott Smither 11-27-1867 (11-28-1867)   [S]
Jeffers, Riley to Polly Chambers 12-26-1854 12-28-1854   [S]
Jeffers, Samuel to Mary Boshears 4-1-1872 (4-4-1872)   [S]
Jeffers, Stephen to Parizidia Duncan 10-29-1869   [S]
Johnson, George to Sarah (Miss) Hamilton 7-18-1876   [S]
Johnson, Homer to Nannie Gibson 3-11-1878   [S]
Johnson, Joe to Merions Powell 7-14-1879 (7-20-1879) B [S]
Johnson, John to Frankie Daulton 7-23-1867   [S]
Johnson, Thos. H. to Anniah? Gillas 10-24-1870 (11-24-1870)   [S]
Jones, Harrison to Zilpha Strunk 11-6-1859   [S]
Jones, Isaac to Sarah Chitwood 11-24-1865 (11-27-1865)   [S]
Jones, Isham to Nancy Strunk 7-28-1864   [S]
Jones, James to Rachel Stephens 8-9-1866   [S]
Jones, James G. to M. Jane Coffee 11-17-1866   [S]
Jones, John to Samantha Holt 12-10-1874   [S]
Jones, Toney to Lizzie White 2-24-1880 (2-26-1880) B [S]
Keath, William to Martha A. Newels 1-27-1865   [S]
Keeler, Adam to Anna L. Massingale 12-28-1875 (12-30-1875)   [S]
Keeth, Hiram jr. to Nitty J. Childers 8-29-1877 (8-28?-1877)   [S]
Keethly, Jordan J. to Jane Massingale 8-30-1870 (9-1-1870)   [S]
Keeton, Baty to Emily Jane Carson 10-12-1868   [S]
Keeton, C. F. to Sarah Jane Foster 9-6-1874   [S]
Keeton, E. B. to Elizabeth Hatfield 12-9-1866   [S]
Keeton, Ewel to Kizia Hatfield 7-23-1859 (7-26-1859)   [S]
Keeton, Harrison to Jane Coffey 6-15-1870 6-16-1870   [S]
Keeton, Scott to Lenora Stephens 10-10-1875   [S]
Keeton, Scott to Parizidia McDonald 6-21-1876   [S]
Kenedy, Martin to Mary E. Stephens 7-19-1877   [S]
Kidd, G. W. to Lucinda R. White 5-8-1876   [S]
Kidd, William J. to Etta Smith 10-19-1878   [S]
Killby, A. S. to S. A. Ray 1-24-1876 (1-25-1876)   [S]
King, Braxton to Charlotte Cox 8-23-1880   [S]
King, Burell to Sarah Jones 8-17-1872   [S]
King, David to Elizabeth King 8-8-1872   [S]
King, David to Sarah Angel 11-24-1866   [S]
King, Elishia to Rosa Duncan 4-14-1860   [S]
King, Enos to Mary Jane Moses 12-22-1877   [S]
King, Jackson to Polly Stephens 2-11-1869   [S]
King, James W. to Julian McDonald 8-27-1870 (9-1-1870)   [S]
King, Jasper to Kizziah Ross 5-2-1867   [S]
King, John to Sophia Lewallen 11-28-1876 (10?-1-1876)   [S]
King, Kirby to Nancy E. Hatfield 9-27-1866   [S]

Scott County Grooms

King, MSatthew to Weltivia Ross 6-30-1878   [S]
King, Marry to Omy King 5-27-1866   [S]
King, Newton to Susan O. Cecil 9-13-1866   [S]
King, Peter to Haley Ann Boyatt 12-27-1877 (12-28-1877)   [S]
King, Pleasant to Polly Ross 2-17-1877   [S]
King, Thomas M. to Jane King 7-20-1880   [S]
King?, F. M. to Susan Jones 10-20-1878   [S]
Lackey, James S. to Elizabeth Hicks 11-3-1873 11-8-1873   [S]
Lackey, Thomas to Susan Silcox 12-12-1859   [S]
Laird, John to Elizabeth Bunch 10-9-1865   [S]
Laughtts?, William Ellis to Nancy Ann Nelson 2-11-1865   [S]
Law, Michael to Mary Jane Massingale 8-25-1877 (8-26-1877)   [S]
Lawson, Edmonson to Bertha Bowling 7-17-1860 (7-18-1860)   [S]
Lawson, George W. to Sarah Carrol 7-8-1864 (7-10-1864)   [S]
Lawson, Jonathin to Sarah Smither 10-16-1876 (10-19-1876)   [S]
Lawson, Micheal to Susanah Birchfield 10-16-1878   [S]
Lawson, Wm. to Mary Ann Phillipps 9-24-1875 (9-25-1875)   [S]
Lawson, Wm. Robert to Emma Smithy 2-27-1879   [S]
Laxton, Alvin to Samantha J. Penington 8-26-1870 (8-31-1870)   [S]
Laxton, John to Molly Sharp 3-19-1858 3-20-1858   [S]
Laxton, Thomas to Delany Baker 4-12-1876 (4-16-1876)   [S]
Lay, Finly to Rachel Sexton 5-19-1877 (5-20-1877)   [S]
Lay, Henry to Parizidia Smith 4-18-1870 4-25-1870   [S]
Lay, Jackson to Parezidia Hughett 10-19-1872 10-20-1872   [S]
Lay, James to Martha M. Duncan 1-24-1878   [S]
Lay, James to Mary Kidd 10-14-1872   [S]
Lay, Jessie to Julia A. Duncan 2-19-1872 (2-22-1872)   [S]
Lay, John to Tempa J. Sexton 2-15-1874 (5-17-1874)   [S]
Lay, John L. to Elizabeth Baird 10-20-1866 1-3-1867   [S]
Lay, Spencer F. to Elizabeth Honeycutt 11-30-1869 12-5-1869   [S]
Lay, Thomas to Caroline Atkins 3-31-1880 (4-8-1880)   [S]
Lay, William to Jane Carson 7-28-1864   [S]
Lay, William jr. to Elizabeth Hamby 8-26-1868 (8-30-1868)   [S]
Leach, Abriham to Serrilda Stephens 6-14-1874 (6-20-1874)   [S]
Lewallen, A. S. to Nancy McDonald 11-14-1869   [S]
Lewallen, Andrew to Barbra Blevins 3-11-1865   [S]
Lewallen, Cambell to Maledun? Young 10-12-1865   [S]
Lewallen, Ewell to Louisa McCally 3-8-1871 (3-9-1871)   [S]
Lewallen, J. F. to Rhoda A. Scott 9-20-1871 (9-21-1871)   [S]
Lewallen, John to Emily McDonald 12-9-1865   [S]
Lewallen, John to Rebecca Robbins 9-4-1877 (9-6-1877)   [S]
Lewallen, Michael to Florence Sharp 12-2-1859 (12-25-1859)   [S]
Lewallen, Reddin to Malinda Griffith 3-25-1869 (3-29-1869)   [S]
Lewallen, Samuell A. to Anira C. Young 9-6-1879 (9-9-1879)   [S]
Lewallen, W. A. to Nancy Acree 11-12-1875 (11-14-1875)   [S]
Lewallen, William to Elizabeth Hembree 1-10-1870   [S]
Lewallen, William to Sarah Smith 9-18-1877 (9-20-1877)   [S]
Litten, Finly to Lidia Smith 7-31-1876 (8-1-1876)   [S]
Litton, A. L. to Savanah Smith 9-27-1875   [S]
Litton, Ebenezer to Margerett L. Kidd 12-24-1878 (12-26-1878)   [S]
Litton, G. W. to H. E. Terry 9-25-1876 (9-29-1876)   [S]
Litton, J. L. to Elvira Evaline Doss 1-7-1879 (1-10-1879)   [S]
Litton, Jacob to Polly An Ryan 7-31-1866 8-2-1866   [S]
Litton, James L. to Louisa C. Taylor 1-3-1876 (1-13-1876)   [S]

Scott County Grooms

Litton, Nelson to Nancy Brown 12-5-1874 (12-10-1874)   [S]
Litton, Rufus D. to Luretta Chitwood 2-1-1869 (2-18-1869)   [S]
Lockey, James S. to Polly Thompson 9-3-1866 9-4-1866   [S]
Logson, Wm. H. to Mary Ann Marcum 7-15-1869   [S]
Long, Henry to Prissey Ann Chitwood 10-8-1875 (10-10-1875)   [S]
Long, Joseph to Villia Perkapile 3-27-1875 (3-28-1875)   [S]
Long, Wm. H. to Lucinda Trammell 9-7-1869 (9-9-1869)   [S]
Lovett, Elias to Martha Worly 12-20-1878   [S]
Lovett, G. W. to Elizabeth Wasson 7-4-1878   [S]
Lovitt, J. M. to Sarah A. Blankenship 3-28-1875   [S]
Lovlas, William H. to Mary Frances Burnett 9-18-1878 (9-28-1878)   [S]
Low, Alexander to M. J. Massingale 7-17-1869 (7-18-1869)   [S]
Low, Andrew to Elizabeth Hatfield 3-20-1870   [S]
Low, D. E. to Nancy Duncan 3-22-1875   [S]
Low, Henry to Nancy A. Goodman 12-30-1875   [S]
Low, Henry to Patsy Jane Byrd 9-3-1872 9-5-1872   [S]
Low, Hiram to Elizabeth Low 8-24-1874 (8-27-1874)   [S]
Low, James to Elizabeth Hatfield 11-22-1879 (11-23-1879)   [S]
Low, John to Nancy R. Atkins 6-23-1873 6-26-1873   [S]
Low, John to Salina Massingale 10-1-1866   [S]
Low, Joseph to Elizabeth Goodman 9-7-1877 (9--16-1877)   [S]
Low, Phillipp to G. Hembree 5-7-1866 5-10-1866   [S]
Low, Thomas to Sarah Jane Atkins 1-26-1878 (1-28-1878)   [S]
Lowery, William to Allis Ward 4-20-1878   [S]
Loyd, Albert S. to Margerett Chambers 10-27-1859   [S]
Loyd, T. J. to Ferbia Huett 11-20-1867 (11-24-1867)   [S]
Manson, George P. to Missouri A. Quimby 6-27-1875 (7-4-1875)   [S]
Marcim, Calvin to Polleyann Hicks 3-27-1865 (3-30-1865)   [S]
Marcum, Gilbert to Sarah J. Eads 1-20-1871 (1-21-1871)   [S]
Marcum, John to Nancy Smith 12-22-1861   [S]
Marcum, John A. to Arlena Phillipps 1-24-1870 1-27-1870   [S]
Marcum, Josiah to Mary Jane Ellis 12-24-1869 1-2-1870   [S]
Marcum, Josiah to Rosa Daughty 3-12-1877 (3-15-1877)   [S]
Marcum, Reason to Charity Smith 8-6-1866   [S]
Marcum, William to Lucy Phillip 4-21-1859 (4-2?-1859)   [S]
Marcun, Josiozas? to Rittia Cross 9-14-1878 (9-15-1878)   [S]
Marlow, William to Pharizonia McDonald 6-23-1869 (6-24-1869)   [S]
Martin, John to M. Jane Gibson 6-4-1857 6-5-1857   [S]
Mason, Anderson to Sally Ann Low 1-8-1870 1-11-1870   [S]
Massengale, John O. to (bride omitted) 1-29-1863   [S]
Masses, Thomas D. to Delphia S. Strunk 7-18-1877   [S]
Massingale, Henry C. to Parrella Thompson 4-11-1878   [S]
Massingale, John to Mary Low 8-21-1878 (8-25-1878)   [S]
Massingale, John to Rutha Drawn 1-17-1874 (1-18-1874)   [S]
Massingale, Jordan to Louisa Shoopman 7-27-1858 (8-7-1858)   [S]
Massingale, Jordan to Sarah Goodman 9-26-1866   [S]
Massingale, Jordon to Salley Low 8-17-1878 (8-30-1878)   [S]
Massingale, Jourdan to Serrilda Low 1-5-1874 (1-9-1874)   [S]
Mayfield, Peter to Mahala Wirt 8-4-1860   [S]
McBride, William to Emerine Phillipps 11-10-1879   [S]
McCarthy, A. S. to Millie Buttram 3-26-1877 (3-27-1877)   [S]
McCarty, Jerimiah to Martha Davis 8-18-1876   [S]
McCarty, John to Sarah Valentine 3-9-1875   [S]
McCoy, Nathaniel G. to Lizzie C. Young 3-12-1878 (3-13-1878)   [S]

Scott County Grooms

McCoy, Thomas to Leodicea Sharp 7-21-1873   [S]
McCoy, Wm. to Martha Hurtt 11-6-1856 11-7-1856   [S]
McDonald, Allen to Kiziah Strunk 2-15-1877   [S]
McDonald, Elihu to Elizabeth Lewallen 3-15-1855 7-15-1855   [S]
McDonald, Elihue to Anna Foster 1-14-1880 (1-15-1880)   [S]
McDonald, Elihue to Martha Ramsey 4-10-1876   [S]
McDonald, Geo. W. to Sarah E. McDonald 4-28-1879 (4-6?-1879)   [S]
McGee, Thomas to Sarah Low 11-7-1860   [S]
McGerr, Edward to Mandy More 5-11-1875   [S]
McIntire, Thomas to Lena Strunk 7-3-1880   [S]
McIntyre, Thomas to Elizabeth Trammell 10-10-1879   [S]
Meadors, David E. to Malinda Moses 7-16-1874   [S]
Meadors, J. J. to Cora Herdle 7-30-1880 (7-23?-1880)   [S]
Meadors, Job to Helen Creekmor 3-3-1856   [S]
Meadors, Joel to Elizabeth Taylor 12-25-1871   [S]
Meadors, Nelson to Nancy Strunk 2-1-1880   [S]
Meadors, Reuben to Sarah J. Wood 12-2-1874 (12-27-1874)   [S]
Meadors, Thomas E. to Gemima Johnson 1-16-1858   [S]
Meal, Geog. W. to Catharine Huff 9-14-1880 (8?-14-1880)   [S]
Mellin, Martin to Mary Ann Muse 12-20-1866   [S]
Merony, Wright to Elizabeth Duncan 7-25-1874 (7-26-1874)   [S]
Miles, Ervin to Catharine Moonyham 10-19-1877 (10-27-1877)   [S]
Miles, Thomas to Sally Ann Reed 5-29-1879   B [S]
Miles, W. C. to E. A. Bodkins 8-25-1876   [S]
Milican, William to Sarah Burk 9-6-1865   [S]
Miller, F. M. to Elizabeth Spradling 4-24-1876 (4-26-1876)   [S]
Miller, James M. to Mary Goad 2-1-1864 (2-2-1864)   [S]
Miller, Robert to Nancy Ann Williams 1-11-1879 (1-12-1879)   [S]
Miller, William to Rebecca Lawson 11-8-1860   [S]
Mills, Alexander to Rutha Hammock 3-13-1877 (3-4?-1877)   [S]
Minton, Robert to Pegga Stephens 6-2-1858   [S]
Mixon, David to Martha Sharp 8-29-1876 (8-30-1876)   [S]
Moffit, Thomas to Elizabeth Young 3-19-1879 (3-23-1879)   [S]
Moffit, Thomas to Elizabeth Young 3-19-1879 (3-28-1879)   [S]
Mohollon, John to Roziah Lewallen 8-10-1869 (8-12-1869)   [S]
Moore, J. W. to Elizabeth Claxton 9-1-1880   [S]
Moore, Napolian to Almedia Holt 8-29-1876 (8-28?-1876)   [S]
More, Elias to Surprony Lovett 6-23-1856   [S]
More, Granville to Elizabeth Meadors 2-14-1859   [S]
More, J. W. to Abigail Hickombottom 5-17-1877   [S]
More, Wesley H. to Nancy Jane Evins 1-28-1866 (1-18?-1866)   [S]
Morow, Thomas to Jane Caroll 10-27-1879   [S]
Morris, James to Louisa Sharp 10-26-1872 10-27-1872   [S]
Morris, Wm. to M. A. Turner 5-3-1876   [S]
Moses, Joshua to Polly Strunk 11-10-1870 (11-24-1870)   [S]
Mosier, Pleasant to Clartine Garner 8-31-1856   [S]
Mounts, Matthew to Milly J. Calhoun 1-14-1878   [S]
Murphy, Abraham to Helen Lay 7-19-1879   [S]
Murphy, David to Rachel Reed 11-17-1864   [S]
Murphy, Joshua to Susan Burk 8-13-1869 (8-15-1869)   [S]
Murphy, Marion to Lucinda Strunk 4-4-1870 4-7-1870   [S]
Murphy, Miles C. to Samantha J. Stephens 1-19-1871   [S]
Murphy, Uriah to Nancy Lay 2-6-1872   [S]
Murphy, W. F. to Isabell M. Smiddy 5-3-1875 (5-9-1875)   [S]

Scott County Grooms

Murphy, William H. to Dorcas Vanover 3-14-1861   [S]
Nathan, John to Elizabeth Wilson 11-3-1872   [S]
Neal, Daniel to Louiza Hatfield 12-24-1867 (12-26-1867)   [S]
Neal, J. S. to Nancy E. Perry 3-3-1878   [S]
Neal, Jacob to Nancy J. Byrd 2-11-1871 (2-12-1871)   [S]
Neal, Jeptha to Mary E. Bruss 7-28-1872   [S]
Neal, T. R. to Sarah A. Hays 5-9-1878   [S]
Nevels, John Wm. to Lucy Ann Noe 6-27-1871   [S]
Newport, Alberson to Mary Griffith 3-23-1874 (3-2?-1874)   [S]
Newport, C. C. to Mary E. Walden 5-17-1878 (5-18-1878)   [S]
Newport, Esau to Mary Jeffers 10-19-1874 (10-22-1874)   [S]
Newport, Ezekial to Clemantine Shoemaker 11-3-1870 (11-6-1870)   [S]
Newport, Ezekial to Nancy Smith 11-22-1860   [S]
Newport, Feelin to Margerett Jeffers 9-19-1859   [S]
Newport, J. H. to Rhoda Ellis 11-20-1877 (11-23-1877)   [S]
Newport, James to Scyrene Hurtt 7-6-1867 7-7-1867   [S]
Newport, James M. to Elizabeth Sharp 1-25-1872 (2-12-1872)   [S]
Newport, James M. to Rebecca Newport 12-5-1878   [S]
Newport, John to Deliah Brown 2-22-1870 2-24-1870   [S]
Newport, John W. to Rachel Hughett 1-3-1876 (1-6-1876)   [S]
Newport, Melvin to Mandy Hughett 3-4-1878 (3-7-1878)   [S]
Newport, Phoenix to Mary Phillipps 10-10-1876 (10-12-1876)   [S]
Newport, Phoenix to Polly Ann Smither 12-29-1868 (1-3-1869)   [S]
Newport, Samuel to Emeline Sexton 7-2-1873 7-3-1873   [S]
Newport, Solomon to Tempa Macart 10-19-1870 (10-20-1870)   [S]
Newport, Thomas to Rebecca Griffith 12-23-1876 (12-28-1876)   [S]
Newport, William to Rachel Mira? Buttram 3-14-1868 (3-19-1868)   [S]
Newport, William jr. to Kiziah Ann Thompson 10-10-1867   [S]
Newport, Wm. to Sereptia Brown 3-30-1867   [S]
Newport, Zekial to Eliza Jane Reed 8-19-1854 8-17-1854?   [S]
Noe, Henry to Margerett Jones 3-9-1880   [S]
O'Brian, Patrick to Rena Strunk 7-25-1875   [S]
Oliver, W. R. to Maggie Dobbs 10-25-1879   [S]
Omara, James M. to Kate Frazier 5-26-1880 (5-21?-1880)   [S]
Overton, Franklin to Mary C. R. E. Wilson 3-10-1879 (3-13-1879)   [S]
Overton, Franklin to Rebecca E. Wilson 10-11-1867 (10-12-1867)   [S]
Overton, John to Nancy Emeline Gosling 3-30-1867   [S]
Overton, William to Martha Overton 7-24-1878 (7-26-1878)   [S]
Overton, William to Rebecca Hembree 4-24-1876 (4-30-1876)   [S]
Owens, Baley to Betty Crabtree 12-4-1855   [S]
Ownes, George W. to Jane Pemberton 5-20-1869 (5-23-1869)   [S]
Ownes, John to Mary S. Acres 5-3-1869   [S]
Ownes, W. W. to Susan J. Penington 7-27-1877 (7-28-1877)   [S]
Ownes, Willis to Sarah Ann Ellis 2-29-1872   [S]
Parker, Alvin to Rhoda A. Potter 9-7-1870 (9-8-1870)   [S]
Parker, Balam C. to Sarah H. Cross 7-5-1873 7-6-1873   [S]
Parker, Columbus to Missouri Todd 7-15-1879 (7-17-1879)   [S]
Parker, Granville to Mary Griffith 4-18-1878   [S]
Parker, James to Susan Duncan 6-16-1856 6-27-1856   [S]
Parker, John to Rachel Thomas 7-15-1880   [S]
Parker, Martin to Sarah Smither 6-13-1870   [S]
Parker, Newton R. to Theny J. Anderson 5-14-1877   [S]
Parker, William to Nancy Shoopman 7-3-1872   [S]
Parker, William Emberson to Elizabeth Silcox 10-10-1859 (10-13-1859)   [S]

Scott County Grooms

Parker, William h. to Saphrano F. Burk 9-17-1874   [S]
Parsons, J. W. to Mahulda Foster 4-3-1880 (4-4-1880)   [S]
Peak, Lenord to Vetha Frances Young 8-10-1877 (8-11-1877)   [S]
Pemberton, George W. to Catharine J. (Miss) Goad 7-17-1876 (7-20-1876)   [S]
Pemberton, James H. to Catharine Cross 9-28-1867 9-29-1867   [S]
Pemberton, James H. to Rebecca Griffith 3-4-1878 (3-7-1878)   [S]
Pemberton, Jefferson to Sarah Anne Sexton 1-8-1863   [S]
Pemberton, Jefferson Cummings to Emiline (Miss) Webb 12-29-1877 (1-2-1878)[S]
Pemberton, Richard to Masha Buttram 7-27-1876   [S]
Pemberton, Richard to Sarah Adkins 7-12-1865   [S]
Pemberton, Richard to Sarah Shoopman 3-5-1878   [S]
Pemberton, Timothy to Lyda McCart 3-10-1873   [S]
Penington, Daniel to Pegga Muse 7-7-1866 7-10-1866   [S]
Penington, G. W. to Arraney Jeffers 10-14-1875   [S]
Penington, James M. to Salley Thompson 7-5-1866   [S]
Penington, James M. to Sally Thompson 7-5-1866   [S]
Penington, Martin to Emerine Slaven 3-19-1880 (3-20-1880)   [S]
Penington, William T. to Ellen Smith 6-23-1867   [S]
Pennington, James M. to E. A. Blakely 11-18-1871 (11-19-1871)   [S]
Perkins, Eligiah to Sarah Jane Mills 5-21-1863 (5-22-1863)   [S]
Perkins, Frank A. to Martha A. Hutson 5-9-1878   [S]
Perkins, James to Nancy Coffey 7-30-1859   [S]
Perkins, Jobe to Frankie R. Shepherd 11-29-1877   [S]
Perkins, Lewis to Rhody Coffey 3-21-1861   [S]
Perkins, William to Martha Gibson 3-9-1876   [S]
Perry, David to Sarrah Vanover 4-4-1855   [S]
Perry, Eli to Mary Jane Long 12-9-1874 (12-10-1874)   [S]
Perry, Eli to Susia J. Perker 5-1-1879   [S]
Perry, Henry to Hiley Ownes 8-29-1876 (8-31-1876)   [S]
Perry, Milfred to Luverna Rose 2-29-1876 (3-1-1876)   [S]
Perry, Nathan to Lucretia Davis 10-12-1877 (10-18-1877)   [S]
Perry, Samuell to Milly Ridner 5-1-1880   [S]
Perry, T. C. to Sarah Vanover 5-10-1877   [S]
Perry, William R. to Luaner A. Burnett 8-25-1879   [S]
Perttete, John to Parizidia Atkins 3-20-1855   [S]
Phelps, Andrew F. to Sarah R. Bray 8-27-1876   [S]
Phelps, James H. to Mary E. Clark 8-2-1871 (8-20-1871)   [S]
Phillipps, Abner to Mary Fine? McDonald 1-16-1866 (1-17-1866)   [S]
Phillipps, Blagbun L. to Salina Cecil 2-11-1880 (2-15-1880)   [S]
Phillipps, Charles to Sarah Foster 2-11-1868 (2-13-1868)   [S]
Phillipps, E. W. to F. J. Cecil 9-29-1876 (9-28?-1876)   [S]
Phillipps, Elswick to Pegga Phillipps 11-2-1872 11-3-1872   [S]
Phillipps, Emanuel to Jane Sephens 3-7-1859   [S]
Phillipps, Emanuell to Pherbia Marcum 9-22-1874 (9-21?-1874)   [S]
Phillipps, Ewell to Franky Litton 7-5-1879   [S]
Phillipps, General to Emily Ellis 2-19-1872 (2-22-1872)   [S]
Phillipps, Ingram to Malinda Griffith 3-6-1878 (3-10-1878)   [S]
Phillipps, James G. to Partily P. Sexton 4-3-1876 (4-6-1876)   [S]
Phillipps, James L. to Elizabeth Robbins 2-8-1875 (2-11-1875)   [S]
Phillipps, Jasper M. to Jane Phillipps 2-4-1874   [S]
Phillipps, John M. to Crelda J. Parker 7-30-1875   [S]
Phillipps, John R. to Winny Marcum 12-15-1874 (12-17-1874)   [S]
Phillipps, John Riley to Rebecca J. Thompson 8-29-1871 (8-31-1871)   [S]
Phillipps, John Scott to Mandy Sexton 10-30-1867 (11-3-1867)   [S]

Scott County Grooms

Phillipps, John W. to Vicy Newport 4-13-1867   [S]
Phillipps, Jonathin to Martha A. Reed 2-3-1869 (2-4-1869)   [S]
Phillipps, Jonathin to Sarah Boyatt 11-4-1878   [S]
Phillipps, Joseph to Lucinda Morgan 8-22-1876   [S]
Phillipps, Josiah to Rebecca Reed 8-1-1870 8-25-1870   [S]
Phillipps, Pleasant W. to Emely C. Cecil 2-17-1869 (2-18-1869)   [S]
Phillipps, Riley to Elizabeth A. Chitwood 10-5-1867 10-9-1867   [S]
Phillipps, Riley to Makiley Partely Atkins 6-5-1854 6-11-1854   [S]
Phillipps, Thomas L. to Nancy J. Newport 4-4-1871   [S]
Phillipps, Whiticar to R. J. Trammell 12-28-1874   [S]
Phillipps, William to Elizabeth Daughty 3-21-1857 7-25-1857   [S]
Phillipps, Winfield S. to Clerinda Parker 5-4-1872   [S]
Phillipps, Wm. J. to Sarah McDonald 1-1-1876 (1-2-1876)   [S]
Phillips, Fountain to Sarah Ellis 7-19-1865 (7-20-1865)   [S]
Phillips, Jonathon to Jane Chitwood 4-4-1859 (4-8-1859)   [S]
Phillips, Robert to Pheba Jane Thompson 3-29-1866   [S]
Potter, J. A. to Margerett Chambers 11-15-1876 (11-16-1876)   [S]
Potter, Julen to Rhoda Buttram 8-25-1855 8-26-1855   [S]
Potter, Julian F. to Nancy E. Chambers 4-2-1878 (4-4-1878)   [S]
Potter, W. M. H. to Charity Chambers 12-31-1873 (1-1-1874)   [S]
Preins?, Califer to Sallie Lessler 12-8-1879   [S]
Price, Robert to Esther Griffith 10-22-1867   [S]
Privett, Hiram to Malinda Rose 12-25-1866   [S]
Rast, Sirens to Dolly Williams 5-7-1854   [S]
Redman, J. R. O. to Mary E. Todd 10-22-1877 (10-20?-1877)   [S]
Redman, M. F. to Florida M. Boehm 5-4-1878 (5-8-1878)   [S]
Redmon, William H. to Emily C. Smith 11-7-1860 (11-8-1860)   [S]
Reed, Adam C. to Victoria Dobbs 10-25-1879   [S]
Reed, Andrew to Polly Ann Carson 12-14-1866 12-19-1866   [S]
Reed, Harrison to Mary Ann Sexton 12-2-1865 (12-3-1865)   [S]
Reed, Isaac to Rachel Ellis 1-30-1878 (1-31-1878)   [S]
Reed, Isaac to Visa Wallice 9-15-1873 9-18-1873   [S]
Reed, J. C. to Emily Smith 3-1-1871 (3-2-1871)   [S]
Reed, John to Pernely Bowling 3-18-1862   [S]
Reed, John to Tabitha C. Massingale 5-29-1860 (6-2-1860)   [S]
Reed, John jr. to Lucinda Parker 9-4-1879   [S]
Reed, Sampson to Angenetty Phillipps 12-21-1874 (12-31-1874)   [S]
Reed, Sampson to Eliza Jayne Thompson 7-13-1864 (7-14-1864)   [S]
Reed, Sampson to Sarah Phillipps 5-18-1873 7-1-1873   [S]
Reynolds, James P. to L. E. Burkhart 8-11-1880   [S]
Reynolds, Major to Louisa Watters 10-25-1860   [S]
Rice, John to Mahala Wilson 11-11-1864   [S]
Richmond, Joseph to Sarah E. Davis 1-23-1880   [S]
Ridenor, Henry B. to Tempa E. Richardson 1-14-1867   [S]
Riggs, William to Martha Cox 5-2-1875   [S]
Risden, B. L. to Millie McDonald 11-4-1875   [S]
Risden, Isaac to Jane Shoopman 1-25-1855   [S]
Risden, J.? M. to Malinda Smither 9-27-1879 (9-28-1879)   [S]
Risden, Jesse to Ithema Terry 10-29-1858 (11-2-1858)   [S]
Risden, Jessie to Anna Davis 12-26-1875 (12-25?-1875)   [S]
Risden, Jobias to Martha A. Chambers 1-18-1878 (1-20-1878)   [S]
Risden, William R. to Catharine Sweet 8-4-1877 (8-5-1877)   [S]
Risden, Wm. to Maryan Byrd 2-18-1856   [S]
Roach, Archibald to Tabbitha Troxwell 10-30-1880   [S]

Scott County Grooms

Robbins, Calvin to Sarah A. Griffith 5-20-1875   [S]
Robbins, Macy to Nettie Godsey 12-25-1879   [S]
Robbins, Michel to Orlena Sexton 10-24-1878 (10-21?-1878)   [S]
Robbins, W. L. to Susana Fry 10-22-1875   [S]
Roberds, S. W.? G. to Amelia Freeman 4-11-1879   [S]
Roberson, Jacob to Surreptia Cross 7-11-1855 7-13-1855   [S]
Roberson, Joel to Surreptia Cross 9-11-1856 9-13-1856   [S]
Roberts, Baly to Nancy Strunk 3-16-1856   [S]
Roberts, Tolbert to Relda Troxwell 9-31-1880 (10-30-1880)   [S]
Robinson, John C. to Drucilla Loyd 12-28-1850 1-1-1851   [S]
Ross, Hamble A. to Mary M. Smith 9-4-1856   [S]
Ross, J. C. to Nancy King 4-28-1878   [S]
Ross, James C. to Jane Meadors 2-26-1857   [S]
Ross, Perleman to Sally Duncan 8-9-1879 (8-10-1879)   [S]
Ross, Thomas to Nancy Tramell 11-14-1879   [S]
Ross, William to Polly King 8-13-1866   [S]
Rosser, J. W. to E. A. Blevins 12-28-1875 (12-30-1875)   [S]
Rosser, John to Gilla Parker 10-17-1859 (10-27-1859)   [S]
Rosser, M. F. to Abigail Cecil 4-3-1880 (4-8-1880)   [S]
Rosser, William to Anna Litton 11-4-1870 (11-10-1870)   [S]
Rosser, William to Rebecca Keeton 9-21-1871   [S]
Roysden, John to Rachel Hamby 11-29-1866   [S]
Russle, Alex to Adaline McClain 7-22-1880 B [S]
Russle, William C. to C. J. Lewallen 4-3-1875 (4-4-1875)   [S]
Ruthford, Jacob to Emeline Foster 4-14-1880   [S]
Ryan, David to Bashaby Harmon 9-25-1866   [S]
Ryan, David to Nancy E. Hays 8-11-1869   [S]
Ryan, David to Relda J. Parker 4-18-1872   [S]
Sanders, Dock to Sarah (Miss) Hill 9-11-1877 (9-13-1877)   [S]
Sanders, Joseph D. W. to Mary Cross 6-1-1880 (6-13-1880)   [S]
Satlaney, James to Jane Ann Parcins 6-15-1860   [S]
Scott, William J. to Martha Jones 6-28-1866   [S]
Sebers, John S. to Reptia Ezrie Barnett 3-31-1879   [S]
Sego, Wm. to Rebecca Parton 1-7-1858 (1-27-1858)   [S]
Seiler?, Jacob to Luisa Newell 8-18-1868   [S]
Sellars, James Henry to Caroline Sumner 12-6-1867   [S]
Sexton, C. C. to Nancy Phillipp 1-17-1868   [S]
Sexton, Daniel to Rebecca Thomas 4-6-1868 (4-8-1868)   [S]
Sexton, David to Calfernia Marcum 8-1-1870 8-8-1870   [S]
Sexton, Eligiah to Melvina E. Parker 1-1-1880 (1-2-1880)   [S]
Sexton, Emanuell to Almiria Brown 9-28-1877 (9-30-1877)   [S]
Sexton, Hiriam to Sophia Griffith 2-26-1858 (3-2-1858)   [S]
Sexton, James to Mary Ann Phillipps 9-27-1862 (10-2-1862)   [S]
Sexton, John to Ester Phillipps 1-1-1855 1-4-1855   [S]
Sexton, John B. to Sarah Phillipps 3-3-1870   [S]
Sexton, Levi to Rosa Jane Ridenour 11-6-1877   [S]
Sexton, Marion to Emeline Newport 11-18-1868 (11-19-1868)   [S]
Sexton, Ransom to Falby Smith 6-25-1871 (6-28-1871)   [S]
Sexton, Riley to Elizabeth Griffith 5-6-1875   [S]
Sexton, Riley to Martha Begley 11-16-1870 (11-17-1870)   [S]
Sexton, Robert to Lucinda Hughett 8-26-1871 (8-31-1871)   [S]
Sexton, Thomas to Nancy Jane Goad 9-24-1866 9-25-1866   [S]
Sexton, William S. to Julian Newport 12-26-1868 (12-27-1868)   [S]
Sexton, William T. to Prissillia Newport 3-11-1873 3-13-1873   [S]

Scott County Grooms

Sexton, Wright to Rachel Foster 12-2-1860   [S]
Sharp, Barney to Susanna Duglass 2-11-1875   [S]
Sharp, Eli to Mary Foust 10-19-1869 10-21-1869 [S]
Sharp, George W. to Elizabeth Dagley 9-22-1869 (9-23-1869) [S]
Sharp, Isham R. to Leander Sexton 10-14-1870   [S]
Sharp, James to Tempy Cross 12-6-1854 12-7-1854   [S]
Sharp, John to Leodica Sharp 2-27-1874 (2-28-1874)   [S]
Sharp, L. D. to Silvania Thompson 9-11-1880 (7?-30-1880)   [S]
Sharp, Nicholas Micheal to E. J. Hill 1-7-1879   [S]
Sharp, Sterling to Delphia Penington 11-27-1876 (11-30-1876)   [S]
Shepherd, Granvill M. to Permelia Stephens 12-21-1865   [S]
Shepherd, John to Susan Wilson 5-29-1870 5-30-1870   [S]
Shoopman, Jacob to Mary Duncan 5-10-1856 5-11-1856   [S]
Shoopman, Milton to Sabry Massingale 9-2-1859 (9-15-1859)   [S]
Silcox, Joseph to Emily A. Boshears 10-23-1867 (10-27-1867)   [S]
Silcox, Levi to Margarett Brummett 1-9-1866 (1-11-1866)   [S]
Silcox, Stephen to Moumen Cook 3-6-1868 (3-8-1868)   [S]
Siler, Joseph to Eliza J. Trammell 4-25-1875 (6-25-1875)   [S]
Siler, Newton to Barbary Osbern 10-3-1880   [S]
Silvers, James W. to Mary Jane Lewis 3-5-1869   [S]
Simpson, Joseph to Lucinda Litton 7-27-1869   [S]
Simpson, Robert to Mary Chitwood 7-23-1869 (7-25-1869)   [S]
Simpson?, Joseph A. to Nancy Jane Fowce 3-5-1866   [S]
Slaven, Anderson to Rhoda Linton Brown 10-17-1861   [S]
Slaven, Andrew to Relda J. Slaven 7-8-1874 (7-9-1874)   [S]
Slaven, E. M. to Seally? Milican 1-25-1866   [S]
Slaven, Geog? W. to Mary A. Emmett 8-17-1870   [S]
Slaven, Granvill to Ary Smith 9-6-1866   [S]
Slaven, J. W. to Mary Blevins 3-22-1866   [S]
Slaven, James to Nancy Stephens 4-2-1857   [S]
Slaven, James G. to Elizabeth (Miss) Pennington 5-22-1878 (5-23-1878)   [S]
Slaven, John to Elizabeth Smith 4-19-1860   [S]
Slaven, John to Rachel Slaven 11-19-1875   [S]
Slaven, Johnathin to Salley Phillipps 4-14-1856   [S]
Slaven, Peter to Margurett Boyatt 2-15-1871 (2-12?-1871)   [S]
Slaven, Richard to M. J. Spradling 3-7-1867   [S]
Slaven, Steward to Sarah Miller 7-27-1872   [S]
Slaven, William to Polley Jane Foster 11-17-1865   [S]
Slaven, William to Polly Slaven 4-15-1878 (4-17-1878)   [S]
Sloan, W. H. to Nancy D. Soloman 2-13-1877   [S]
Small, D. C. to E. Childers 10-5-1875   [S]
Smith, Ali to Mary Young 3-3-1880   [S]
Smith, C. C. to Elvira Brown 9-20-1875 (9-23-1875)   [S]
Smith, Calvin to Emily Ownes 2-28-1874 (3-1-1874)   [S]
Smith, David to Mandy Litton 12-8-1874 (12-12-1874)   [S]
Smith, Edward to Sarah J. Ross 10-25-1866   [S]
Smith, Ewell to Luverna Marcum 4-2-1866   [S]
Smith, G. W. to M. W. Slaven 9-23-1869   [S]
Smith, George to Emily Thomas 6-3-1869   [S]
Smith, Harmon to Rhoda Ann Foster 4-5-1877   [S]
Smith, Harrison to Fanny Cotton 4-1-1876 (4-5-1876)   [S]
Smith, J. R. to Mary E. Jardon 10-20-1875 (10-22-1875)   [S]
Smith, J. T. to Sarah Reed 3-22-1869 (3-26-1869)   [S]
Smith, J. T. to Sarah Reed 3-22-1869 (3-26-1869)   [S]

Scott County Grooms

Smith, J. W. to Luiza Humty? 8-7-1862   [S]
Smith, Jackson to Rebecca Thomas 1-31-1855 2-2-1855   [S]
Smith, Jackson G. to Malinda Terry 5-19-1860 (5-20-1860)   [S]
Smith, James to Rebecca Owens 2-3-1863   [S]
Smith, James to Sarah Jane Low 4-15-1880   [S]
Smith, James to Scharlott Miller 4-26-1880   [S]
Smith, James A. to Luanner J. Chambers 3-1-1876 (3-2-1876)   [S]
Smith, James F. to Mattie Wimberley 3-3-1881   [S]
Smith, Jasper to Mary Steeley 9-27-1879   [S]
Smith, John to Agga Richard 2-2-1865   [S]
Smith, John to Manda J. Pennington 11-7-1870   [S]
Smith, John to Nancy Sweet 4-13-1859   [S]
Smith, Jonathan to Lora E. Roberts 9-25-1858 9-30-1858   [S]
Smith, Jonathin to Sarah Newport 1-23-1860   [S]
Smith, Joshua to Martha M. Parker 9-3-1879 (9-4-1879)   [S]
Smith, Riley to Mary E. Crabtree 12-11-1877   [S]
Smith, S. to Linda Hurtt 3-31-1855 4-1-1855   [S]
Smith, Samuel to Charity Draughn 5-10-1873 5-12-1873   [S]
Smith, Stephen to Jayne Overton 3-2-1865 (3-6-1865)   [S]
Smith, W. A. to Mary E. Taylor 4-1-1875   [S]
Smith, William to Lakey Chitwood 11-17-1876 (11-19-1876)   [S]
Smith, William to Nancy Fox 2-5-1860   [S]
Smith, William to Rhoda Sexton 3-27-1861 (4-7-1861)   [S]
Smith, William to Rutha Meadors 7-19-1874   [S]
Smith, William jr. to Sarah West 9-17-1876 (9-23-1876)   [S]
Smith, Wm. R. to Pernetta Anderson 9-30-1879   [S]
Smither, Jessie to L. E. Wilson 8-7-1878 (8-18-1878)   [S]
Smither, Jessie to Luesy Shoemaker 9-2-1867 9-3-1867   [S]
Smither, Reuben to Martha Thompson 4-12-1874   [S]
Smither, Thomas to Mary Brooks 10-3-1865 (10-4-1865)   [S]
Smither, William to Lucindia Parker 11-10-1879   [S]
Solomon, Robert P. to Elizabeth Powell 12-18-1877   [S]
Sommers, B. L. to Anna Redmon 9-11-1860   [S]
Spradling, Abner W. to Rachel King 4-23-1880 (7-23-1880)   [S]
Spradling, Anderson to Synthia Stephens 9-14-1865   [S]
Spradling, Isam to N. E. Winchester 8-18-1876   [S]
Spradling, Pleasant to Nancy Coffey 3-30-1861   [S]
Spradling, William to Polly Manning 7-7-1878   [S]
Spradling, William to Susan Winchester 4-27-1867   [S]
Springfield, Willis to Lucretia Scarberry 11-19-1880   [S]
Stanfill, Sampson to Elizabeth Smith 5-18-1867 5-19-1867   [S]
Stanley, Ewell to Lucinda Chitwood 12-21-1876 (12-28-1876)   [S]
Stanley, James to Burtha Dagley 12-31-1860 (1-2-1861)   [S]
Stanley, Rhodes to Nancy Trammell 5-19-1872   [S]
Stanley, Robert to Sally Ann Carson 2-2-1872 (2-8-1872)   [S]
Stanley, Robert jr. to Luvamer Jane Ownes 1-10-1872 (1-12-1872)   [S]
Stanly, David to Marylin Daughty 11-10-1878 (11-17-1878)   [S]
Stanly, Feril H. to Mahulda Ellott 4-18-1861 (4-21-1861)   [S]
Stanly, Robert to Emily Cobb 3-14-1879 (3-23-1879)   [S]
Stephens, Alvin to Lica Cordell 2-20-1862   [S]
Stephens, Andrrew to Eliza Childres 5-15-1877   [S]
Stephens, Critenden to Catharine Vanover 3-26-1877 (3?-1-1877)   [S]
Stephens, David to Nancy Taylor 8-28-1872   [S]
Stephens, Doswell to Catharine West 11-7-1869   [S]

Scott County Grooms

Stephens, Gabrel to Sarelda J. Barnett 6-28-1876   [S]
Stephens, Granville to Sarah Cordell 4-12-1856 4-15-1856   [S]
Stephens, Henry T. to Rachel Lay 8-21-1878 (8-29-1878)   [S]
Stephens, Hiriam to Elizabeth Dagly 4-7-1855 4-8-1855   [S]
Stephens, J. G. to Manerva Ross 1-26-1856 2-26-1856   [S]
Stephens, James to Mary Vanover 12-25-1876 (12-23?-1876)   [S]
Stephens, Jeptha to Martha Laxton 2-1-1867 2-14-1867   [S]
Stephens, Joseph to Lucinda Tramell 3-26-1866   [S]
Stephens, Joseph M. to Susa King 11-29-1877   [S]
Stephens, Joshua to Sarah J. Honly 2-1-1872   [S]
Stephens, Marion to M. E. Wilson 3-10-1877   [S]
Stephens, Moses to Florinda Hill 12-27-1860   [S]
Stephens, Noah to Martha An Keeth 12-18-1865   [S]
Stephens, Reuben to Sarilda Strunk 4-10-1860   [S]
Stephens, Soloman to Susan Davis 1-8-1876 (1-9-1876)   [S]
Stephens, Thomas to Elizabeth Spradling 1-11-1860   [S]
Stephens, W. W. to Mary Lay 8-27-1871 8-28-1871   [S]
Stepp, W. M. to Ratty Vincens 12-29-1875 (1-2-1876)   [S]
Stone, John W. to Sarah E. Helton 2-13-1877   [S]
Stonecipher, Curtis to Mary Ann Lewallen 8-13-1872 8-15-1872   [S]
Stonecipher, E. L. to Callie Ladd 9-2-1875   [S]
Stonecipher, James S. to Nancy M. Lewallen 9-2-1875 (9-4-1875)   [S]
Stonecipher, Joseph to Nancy M. Parker 11-19-1867 (11-7?-1867)   [S]
Stover, John to Perlina Dugger 8-13-1870 (8-25-1870)   [S]
Stringfield, George W. to Jane Shoemaker 11-7-1871   [S]
Stringfield, Richard to Lucinda West 12-27-1864   [S]
Strunk, A. J. to Margerett Tramell 5-28-1878 (5-23?-1878)   [S]
Strunk, A. J. to Rosa J. Privett 11-26-1871   [S]
Strunk, Burl to Elizabeth Jones 10-13-1870   [S]
Strunk, D. E. A. to E. J. Cooper 1-9-1875   [S]
Strunk, Emberson to Mary Jane Minton 7-7-1859   [S]
Strunk, Enos to Susana T. Bruce 7-30-1875   [S]
Strunk, G. J. to Rachel King 11-25-1875   [S]
Strunk, G. W. to Dillie McDonald 11-18-1875   [S]
Strunk, G. W. to Lensy Ann King 7-29-1875   [S]
Strunk, Gideon to Martha Taylor 1-2-1862   [S]
Strunk, H. J. to Elizabeth Newport 1-26-1870 1-27-1870   [S]
Strunk, Henry B. to Elizabeth King 3-14-1867   [S]
Strunk, Marion to Catharine Buttram 9-4-1879   [S]
Strunk, Murry to Emily Wilson 1-6-1870   [S]
Strunk, Noah to Sophia Higgenbotham 8-8-1870 (8-14-1870)   [S]
Sumer, Mark to Mary An More 2-25-1860   [S]
Sumner, Jerimier to Malinda Wilson 7-20-1854   [S]
Swain, James H. to Mary L. Stephens 8-24-1879 (8-25-1879)   [S]
Swain, S. J. to Eliza A. Kidd 3-18-1877   [S]
Swain, Shelby to Barbara Ann Jourdan 12-31-1866   [S]
Sweet, James to Sarah Smith 7-21-1859   [S]
Swiney, M. to Bridgett Curgis 3-28-1875   [S]
Tapley, William to Elizabeth Douglass 2-28-1867 3-28-1867   [S]
Tassel?, J. C. B. to Rachel Smith 11-23-1879   [S]
Taylor, Alvin to Seala Elreath 9-7-1866   [S]
Taylor, Britton to Lucy Ann Brown 9-8-1866 9-11-1866   [S]
Taylor, Isaac to Nancy Sexton 7-4-1880 (7-5-1880)   [S]
Taylor, John to Mary Dyer 3-5-1878 (3-8-1878)   [S]

Scott County Grooms

Taylor, Reuben to Elizabeth Cooper 1-4-1872   [S]
Taylor, Thomas to Nancy Jane Perry 5-26-1879 (5-30-1879)   [S]
Taylor, William to M. A. Vanover 8-11-1877   [S]
Terrill, Harrison to Margarett Madern 8-17-1867 10-16-1867   [S]
Terry, Calvin to Rutha Slaven 1-21-1856 1-24-1856   [S]
Terry, Eligiah to Sylva Strunk 7-29-1866   [S]
Terry, Haron to Artema Coill 8-1-1865   [S]
Terry, Marion to Harriett Smith 8-19-1865 (8-22-1865)   [S]
Terry, Marion to Patsy Ann Smither 6-26-1878 (7-7-1878)   [S]
Terry, Martin to Sarah Bowlin 11-11-1865   [S]
Terry?, Martin to Lurana Marcum 6-1-1865 (6-3-1865)   [S]
Thomas, Andrew to Nancy West 10-16-1879   [S]
Thomas, Calaway to Drusey Sharp 1-23-1878 (1-24-1878)   [S]
Thomas, Calvin to Elizabeth Foster 2-1-1869 (2-11-1869)   [S]
Thomas, Isaac to Emeline Thomas 4-2-1872 (4-4-1872)   [S]
Thomas, John to F. E. Chambers 9-23-1880   [S]
Thomas, Reuben to Kiziar Hatfield 10-25-1875   [S]
Thomas, W. F. to Deliah Reed 3-15-1877   [S]
Thomas, William to Anna Hammock 11-3-1860 (11-4-1860)   [S]
Thomas, William to Catharine E. Ross 9-26-1866   [S]
Thompson, A. J. to Nancy L. Phillipps 8-24-1865   [S]
Thompson, Andrew to Elizabeth Trammell 3-17-1869 (4-1-1869)   [S]
Thompson, Blagburn to Kizzia Ann Phillips 11-18-1860   [S]
Thompson, Elswick to Clara Jane Buttram 3-20-1868 (3-26-1868)   [S]
Thompson, Elswick to Parisidia Pemberton 1-22-1870 1-27-1870   [S]
Thompson, Esau to Parazidia Buttram 1-4-1869 (1-7-1869)   [S]
Thompson, Geog. Washington to Parizidia West 2-3-1879 (3-6-1879)   [S]
Thompson, Harmon to Elizabeth Cross 1-10-1856   [S]
Thompson, Harmon to Louisa J. Cross 11-22-1873 11-23-1873   [S]
Thompson, Harmon J. to Nancy Byrd 12-2-1872 12-5-1872   [S]
Thompson, Jackson to Lucinda Jeffers 4-26-1856 4-27-1856   [S]
Thompson, Jacob to Martha L. Buttram 2-23-1873   [S]
Thompson, James to Millie Holess 7-21-1877   [S]
Thompson, John to Polly Litton 7-16-1870 7-21-1870   [S]
Thompson, Lewis to M. E. Penington 3-30-1876   [S]
Thompson, Scott to Ella (Miss) Harp 3-16-1878 (3-18-1878)   [S]
Thompson, W. F. to Mary Price 9-1-1880   [S]
Thompson, William L. to Julia A. Sexton 2-2-1880 (2-5-1880)   [S]
Todd, William to Sarah L. Williams 6-23-1874   [S]
Tralwell?, John to Nancy Foster 10-26-1876   [S]
Tramell, D. W. S. to Margarett Emeline Murphy 5-8-1869 (5-11-1869)   [S]
Tramell, Danswell to Polly Chitwood 10-30-1878 (10-31-1878)   [S]
Tramell, Dowswell to Gemima Meadors 6-14-1866   [S]
Tramell, Richard to Martha Stephens 3-30-1860 (5-31-1860)   [S]
Tramell, William E. to Elizabeth Siler 1-4-1880   [S]
Trammell, David to Elizabeth Chitwood 12-25-1868   [S]
Trammell, David to Sarah Honeycutt 12-4-1865 (12-10-1865)   [S]
Trammell, Denis to Viana Luan Bowling 4-8-1873 4-20-1873   [S]
Trammell, Fredrick to Mary S. Crabtree 1-23-1870   [S]
Trammell, James H. to Sarah Angel 3-23-1872 (3-25-1872)   [S]
Trammell, Sterling to Sarah O.? Blankenship 1-5-1878   [S]
Trammell, William to Phobea Brown 12-28-1871   [S]
Troxdall, James D. to Malinda Spradling 12-23-1863   [S]
Troxdell, James Granville to Malinda Spradling 12-23-1863   [S]

Scott County Grooms

Troxel, Joseph to Martha Troxel 6-22-1866   [S]
Troxell, David to Lewrana Foster 9-1-1869   [S]
Troxell, George W. to Marga Foster 9-1-1869   [S]
Troxell, Jacob to Salina Steel 1-1-1866   [S]
Troxwell, George to Elizabeth R. White 11-27-1865   [S]
Troxwell, Hiram to Martha Foster 3-30-1861   [S]
Troxwell, Joseph to Angelina J. Gregory 12-15-1864   [S]
Tucker, johnson to Lucinda Bowling 3-13-1873 3-14-1873   [S]
Vaney, Henenson to Sarah J. Edmonson 10-28-1875 (10-30-1875)   [S]
Vanover, D. H. to Peggy Perry 11-3-1876   [S]
Vanover, Henderson to Margerett Canady 9-27-1878   [S]
Vanover, John to Molly Canady 11-3-1876   [S]
Vanover, M. B. to A. E. Sellars 1-20-1879   [S]
Vanover, Samuel to Eliza Vanover 9-25-1867   [S]
Vanover, Samuell to Emily Berry? 2-2-1868   [S]
Vanover, W. R. to Lutheny New 9-11-1874   [S]
Vaughlin, James to Sarah Lewis 4-6-1879   [S]
Wadkins, Luke to Sylvania Stephens 1-15-1875   [S]
Walker, Daniel to Almirah Goad 3-12-1866   [S]
Walker, Elihu to Marguett Malinda Meadors 9-12-1856   [S]
Walker, Isaac to Polly Ann Hays 2-15-1880   [S]
Walker, James P. to Luvania Duncan 6-16-1856   [S]
Walker, Joseph to Sharlett Berges 12-26-1875   [S]
Walker, Micheal to Polly Goad 10-6-1877   [S]
Walker, Thomas to Emily Sexton 1-6-1879 (1-11-1879)   [S]
Walker, William to Elmiriah Brown 6-13-1874   [S]
Walker, William to Louisa Lewallen 8-19-1871 (8-31-1871)   [S]
Wallace, Isaac to Anna Mallissa Scarberry 6-1-1880 (6-2-1880)   [S]
Wallace, Isaac to Jane Foster 4-19-1870 4-20-1870   [S]
Wallace, Joseph to Susan Commerce 7-29-1861 (7-30-1861)   [S]
Ward, William to Elizabeth Low 6-28-1878 (6-29-1878)   [S]
Warly, Cador to Louisa (Miss) Lovett 10-3-1878 (10-17-1878)   [S]
Wason, John to Elisabeth Strunk 7-17-1879   [S]
Watson, Joiles to Jane Abbott 10-4-1864   [S]
Watson, Robert to Tabbitha Marcum 3-17-1877 (3-27-1877)   [S]
Watter, Moses to Emily Anderson 33-14-1870   [S]
Watters, F. M. to Mary Newport 6-8-1875 (7-20-1875)   [S]
Watters, Moses to Elizabeth Boyatt 2-22-1878 (2-23-1878)   [S]
Wattson, Ail to Eliza Bowlen 2-3-1875   [S]
Wattson, Alvin to Polly Winchester 9-12-1878   [S]
Wattson, Hiram M. to Rebecca J. Upchurch 6-24-1872   [S]
Wattson, Wm. to Sarah Leach 3-4-1876   [S]
Webb, George to Lucinda Thompson 3-23-1871 (4-6-1871)   [S]
Webb, John F. to Anna M. Phillipps 10-11-1874 (10-15-1874)   [S]
Webb, W. D. to Lucy Young 3-27-1876 (3-30-1876)   [S]
Webster, Peter to Mary Jane McKiney 10-7-1876 (10-8-1876)   [S]
West, C. H. to Rozanna Caroll 10-30-1861 (10-31-1861)   [S]
West, C. J. to Rebecca Laxton 12-28-1872 1-2-1873   [S]
West, Charles to Artema Cecil 10-13-1868 (10-15-1868)   [S]
West, Charles to Martha Phillipps 11-13-1864 (11-20-1864)   [S]
West, Charles H. to Rozana Carroll 10-30-1861   [S]
West, Crusoe to Arline Goad 9-11-1877 (9-13-1877)   [S]
West, General Taylor to Nancy Sexton 7-20-1866 7-21-1866   [S]
West, Green Berry to Felaney? Marcum 11-16-1870 (11-17-1870)   [S]

Scott County Grooms

West, Pleasant W. to Emily David 9-24-1873   [S]
West, R. C. to Malinda Smither 10-31-1874 (11-1-1874)   [S]
West, Reason to Nancy Phillipps 5-7-1857   [S]
West, Reason jr. to Nancy Smither 11-20-1867 (11-21-1867)   [S]
West, Reuben to Elizabeth Ellis 8-21-1873 8-24-1873   [S]
West, Ruben to Jennie Smither 7-25-1877 (8-2-1877)   [S]
West, Wesley to Phoeba Chambers 1-18-1870 1-20-1870   [S]
West, William to Crisy Ann Sexton 9-4-1870 (9-8-1870)   [S]
West, William A. to Emely Brassfield 5-4-1854   [S]
Wheeler, Dan to Mahaly Jasper 8-19-1880   [S]
White, Jasper N. to Rutha Parker 1-29-1880   [S]
Whittenburg, James to Tennessee Kincaid 10-2-1879   [S]
Wilchtree, William to Rhoda Ann Helton 11-8-1878   [S]
Wilder, Joel to Nancy Patrick 9-18-1869 9-19-1869   [S]
Willeby, Alfred to Parizidiar Ellirs 10-24-1877 (10-25-1877)   [S]
Willhite, J. C. to Celina Brown 9-7-1869 (9-10-1869)   [S]
Williams, G. W. to Lucinda Hammon 12-24-1877 (12-25-1877)   [S]
Williams, John H. to Mary E. Stephens 2-23-1880   [S]
Williams, W. H. to Pheobe J. Reed 12-25-1879 (12-27-1879)   [S]
Williamson, Arther to Sarah E. Rosser 5-11-1872   [S]
Williby, James to Arbanna Buttram 6-20-1878 (6-21-1878)   [S]
Willson, W. S. to Betty Ann Walker 3-16-1876   [S]
Willson, Willern to Vina Maxwell 10-7-1876   [S]
Willson, William to Rebecca More 2-28-1879   [S]
Wilson, Alexander to Nancy J. Wilson 10-28-1874   [S]
Wilson, Alexander to Nancy J. Wilson 10-28-1874   [S]
Wilson, Edward to Margerett Owens 4-18-1876 (4-20-1876)   [S]
Wilson, Elihue to Louisa Maxwell 10-7-1876   [S]
Wilson, Henry to Sarena C. Moses 10-8-1868   [S]
Wilson, James to Rebecca Morrow 3-20-1870   [S]
Wilson, John to Mary Overton 8-27-1877 (8-29-1877)   [S]
Wilson, John to Mary J. Wilson 10-2-1873   [S]
Wilson, Leroy to Ellen Taylor 10-10-1878   [S]
Wilson, Manuel to Hanah R. Melda Gilbreth 12-1-1861   [S]
Wilson, Mark to nannie Shadoan 8-29-1876   [S]
Wilson, Mathew to Lucinda Moor 1-18-1876 (1-19-1876)   [S]
Wilson, P. L. to Emerine Bryant 1-13-1878   [S]
Wilson, Richard to Anna Stephens 11-17-1870   [S]
Wilson, Sam to Matty Jones 12-24-1877 (12-27-1877)   [S]
Winchester, Joseph to Canzada Spradling 6-14-1878   [S]
Winchester, William to Berthena Foster 2-17-1875   [S]
Wolsey, Benjamin to Margerett Wilson 10-22-1860   [S]
Wolsey, Willis to Rachel Jones 1-5-1866   [S]
Worley, John Wesley to Martha Ann Foster 11-13-1863   [S]
Worley, Willis to Jemmima Shepherd 2-3-1860 (2-4-1860)   [S]
Worll?, James to Martha J. Willson 4-15-1880   [S]
Worly, Elias to Mary Jane Lovett 3-14-1878   [S]
Wright, Dennis C. to Lucinda Angel 7-16-1877   [S]
Wright, H. C. to Sarah A. Angel 4-20-1880   [S]
Wright, James W. to Susan Shoopman 6-26-1878 (6-27-1878)   [S]
Wright, Wiley to Margerett Minton 7-22-1880   [S]
Yancy, Calvin to Julia Ann Sexton 8-6-1877 (8-9-1877)   [S]
York, Andrew to Lucinda Newport 3-16-1870   [S]
York, Calep to Polly Lewallen 5-7-1866   [S]

Scott County Grooms

York, David to Juliann Holdaway 11-7-1867   [S]
York, Jerimiah to Louisa Harness 5-18-1861   [S]
York, Jesse to Emely Jeffers 4-13-1861   [S]
Young, Andrew to Sarah Goad 9-30-1859 (10-2-1859)   [S]
Young, Bardon to Markett F. Johnson 12-21-1865   [S]
Young, G. W. to Mary E. Smith 10-24-1876 (10-26-1876)   [S]
Young, J. B. to Martha F. Peck 12-10-1879   [S]
Young, John to Rebecca Goodan 6-27-1856 6-24-1856?   [S]
Yowden, William to Maria B. Decker 8-26-1879   [S]

Scott County Brides

Abbit, Sarah to Wm. Claxton 9-5-1877 (12-7-1877)
Abbott, Jane to Joiles Watson 10-4-1864
Abbott, Martha E. to Solimon Abbott 3-30-1880 (3-22?-1880)
Abbott, Salaanay to Nimrod Angel 2-15-1866
Acree, Nancy to W. A. Lewallen 11-12-1875 (11-14-1875)
Acres, Kiziah to James E. Gibson 7-4-1870 7-21-1870
Acres, Mary S. to John Ownes 5-3-1869
Adkerson, Nancy to Levi Faron 4-6-1865
Adkerson, Nancy E. to Levy Faron 4-6-1865
Adkins, Sarah to Richard Pemberton 7-12-1865
Allen, Mary to J. L. Braddy 11-18-1875
Alley, Jane to Freelin Gosalin 11-4-1854 11-5-1854
Anderson, Creasanor to John Chambers 12-24-1855 12-25-1855
Anderson, Emily to Moses Watter 33-14-1870
Anderson, Mandy L. to James J. Bruce 1-9-1876 (1-10-1876)
Anderson, Mary to Burton Bird 2-20-1856 2-24-1856
Anderson, Partely to Johnson Gibson 11-10-1877 (11-11-1877)
Anderson, Pernetta to Wm. R. Smith 9-30-1879
Anderson, Rebecca to James Childers 5-1-1879
Anderson, Theny J. to Newton R. Parker 5-14-1877
Angel, Evaline to James Angel 6-4-1877 (6-10-1877)
Angel, Lucinda to Mancil Angel 4-7-1876
Angel, Lucinda to Dennis C. Wright 7-16-1877
Angel, Narcissus to James Angel 7-19-1874
Angel, Sarah to David King 11-24-1866
Angel, Sarah to James H. Trammell 3-23-1872 (3-25-1872)
Angel, Sarah A. to H. C. Wright 4-20-1880
Ann, Nancy to William Ellis Laughtts? Nelson 2-11-1865
Atkins, Caroline to Thomas Lay 3-31-1880 (4-8-1880)
Atkins, Elizabeth to James Claxton 6-5-1874 (6-7-1874)
Atkins, Elizabeth to Rufus Cross 3-5-1878 (3-7-1878)
Atkins, Ellen to Moses F. Hurtt 12-20-1870 (12-22-1870)
Atkins, Louisa? to Alexander Goodman 8-4-1873 8-7-1873
Atkins, Makiley Partely to Riley Phillipps 6-5-1854 6-11-1854
Atkins, Marleny to Joseph Cross 11-8-1873 11-20-1873
Atkins, Nancy R. to John Low 6-23-1873 6-26-1873
Atkins, Parizidia to John Perttete 3-20-1855
Atkins, Samantha J. to Alfred Cross 1-13-1880 (1-17-1880)
Atkins, Sarah Jane to Thomas Low 1-26-1878 (1-28-1878)
Atkins, Tellithia Can to Washington Cooper 8-6-1868
Baird, Elizabeth to John L. Lay 10-20-1866 1-3-1867
Baker, Delany to Thomas Laxton 4-12-1876 (4-16-1876)
Baker, Melda (Miss) to Linsay Chitwood 10-18-1877
Ball, Mahala to J. A. Davenport 10-1-1877 (10-7-1877)
Balloo, Easter to Robert Hardwick 2-20-1861
Barnett, Reptia Ezrie to John S. Sebers 3-31-1879
Barnett, Sarelda J. to Gabrel Stephens 6-28-1876
Batts, Lucinda to Thomas Chambers 1-14-1879 (1-19-1879)
Batts, Sarah to William Ellis 1-27-1876 (1-17?-1876)
Begley, Martha to Riley Sexton 11-16-1870 (11-17-1870)
Begly, Sarah to James C. Hamby 7-27-1874 (8-6-1874)
Bell, Annie to John M. Decker 5-10-1876 (5-12-1876)
Bell, Artymsy to W. H. Grigory 5-27-1878 (5-21?-1878)

Scott County Brides

Berge, Thursy Ann to Elihue Bowline 10-11-1877
Berges, Sharlett to Joseph Walker 12-26-1875
Berry?, Emily to Samuell Vanover 2-2-1868
Birchfield, Susanah to Micheal Lawson 10-16-1878
Birge, Pherby to Ewell Chambers 8-29-1872
Birges, Clara to James Bruce 9-24-1870 (10-16-1870)
Blakely, Angeline to Elihue Chambers 1-18-1876 (1-19-1876)
Blakely, E. A. to James M. Pennington 11-18-1871 (11-19-1871)
Blankenship, Sarah A. to J. M. Lovitt 3-28-1875
Blankenship, Sarah O.? to Sterling Trammell 1-5-1878
Blevins, Barbra to Andrew Lewallen 3-11-1865
Blevins, E. A. to J. W. Rosser 12-28-1875 (12-30-1875)
Blevins, Mary to J. W. Slaven 3-22-1866
Blevins, Mary Jane to G. W. Chitwood 8-24-1869 (8-26-1869)
Blevins, Polly to Elias S. Blevins 1-6-1875
Blevins, Sarah to Lewis Burk 6-11-1868
Blevins, Sarah to Samuell Evins 1-25-1876 (1-27-1876)
Bodkins, E. A. to W. C. Miles 8-25-1876
Boehm, Florida M. to M. F. Redman 5-4-1878 (5-8-1878)
Boshears, Emily A. to Joseph Silcox 10-23-1867 (10-27-1867)
Boshears, Huldy to Wm. R. H. Boshears 9-9-1871 (9-10-1871)
Boshears, Mary to Samuel Jeffers 4-1-1872 (4-4-1872)
Boshears, Omy to James Jeffers 6-11-1870 6-12-1870
Bowlen, Eliza to Ail Wattson 2-3-1875
Bowlen, Sarah to Alfred Gibson 7-29-1879 (7-30-1879)
Bowlin, Jane to John Halmon 8-26-1875 (8-29-1875)
Bowlin, Lucinda to Julin Jeffers 8-29-1878
Bowlin, Sarah to Newton Harness 10-4-1875 (10-13-1875)
Bowlin, Sarah to Martin Terry 11-11-1865
Bowling, Angeline to Emanuell Bowling 3-30-1880 (3-31-1880)
Bowling, Angeline to Calvin Hatfield 11-11-1871
Bowling, Bertha to Edmonson Lawson 7-17-1860 (7-18-1860)
Bowling, Elizabeth to W. H. Cox 10-12-1864
Bowling, Lucinda to johnson Tucker 3-13-1873 3-14-1873
Bowling, Nancy to William Caroll 4-13-1861 (4-14-1861)
Bowling, Pernely to John Reed 3-18-1862
Bowling, Susanah to Samuell Harness 1-7-1879 (1-9-1879)
Bowling, Viana Luan to Denis Trammell 4-8-1873 4-20-1873
Boyatt, Elizabeth to Moses Watters 2-22-1878 (2-23-1878)
Boyatt, Haley Ann to Peter King 12-27-1877 (12-28-1877)
Boyatt, Margurett to Peter Slaven 2-15-1871 (2-12?-1871)
Boyatt, Sarah to Jonathin Phillipps 11-4-1878
Brahears, Martha Jane to Alfred Byrd 4-11-1870
Brantley, Kate to Joshua Bradley 1-2-1880
Brassfield, Emely to William A. West 5-4-1854
Bray, Sarah R. to Andrew F. Phelps 8-27-1876
Bridges, Elizabeth to Thomas Honeycutt 2-21-1860
Bridges, Jane to James G. Eliott 9-1-1873 9-4-1873
Bridges, Nancy to Uriah Honeycutt 10-10-1861
Bridges, Sureptia to Bryant Honeycutt 10-3-1864
Brooks, Mary to Thomas Smither 10-3-1865 (10-4-1865)
Brown, Almiria to Emanuell Sexton 9-28-1877 (9-30-1877)
Brown, Celina to J. C. Willhite 9-7-1869 (9-10-1869)
Brown, Deliah to John Newport 2-22-1870 2-24-1870

Scott County Brides

Brown, Elmiriah to Jerimiah Harness 2-1-1873 2-2-1873
Brown, Elmiriah to William Walker 6-13-1874
Brown, Elvina to William Harness 7-23-1868
Brown, Elvira to C. C. Smith 9-20-1875 (9-23-1875)
Brown, Emely to Anderson Hicks 7-12-1869 (7-13-1869)
Brown, Lucy Ann to Britton Taylor 9-8-1866 9-11-1866
Brown, Mary J. to William Chambers 7-1-1878 (7-4-1878)
Brown, Nancy to Nelson Litton 12-5-1874 (12-10-1874)
Brown, Nancy Jane to Thomas W. Harness 10-11-1865 (10-12-1865)
Brown, Nella to Dauze H. Creekmore 2-14-1878 (2-15-1878)
Brown, Phobea to William Trammell 12-28-1871
Brown, Pollyan to Robin Hughett 6-14-1857
Brown, Rhoda Linton to Anderson Slaven 10-17-1861
Brown, Sereptia to Wm. Newport 3-30-1867
Bruce, Agny to Joseph Hatfield 4-18-1877
Bruce, Susana T. to Enos Strunk 7-30-1875
Brummett, Lisey to Jacob Hendrick 12-24-1875 (12-25-1875)
Brummett, Margarett to Levi Silcox 1-9-1866 (1-11-1866)
Brummit, Lizzie to Joel L. Brooks 3-28-1865 (3-30-1865)
Bruss, Mary E. to Jeptha Neal 7-28-1872
Bryant, Emerine to P. L. Wilson 1-13-1878
Bunch, Barzilia to Ezekiel Hembree ?-15-1865 (3-19-1865)
Bunch, Elizabeth to John Laird 10-9-1865
Burchfield, Elizabeth to Isaac Boshears]4-10-1873
Burchfield, Mary A. to L.? C. Atkins 12-1-1873 12-6-1873
Burgan, Susan E. to William Gaston 8-3-1867
Burk, Almirah to James Dick 2-28-1871
Burk, Saphrano F. to William h. Parker 9-17-1874
Burk, Sarah to William Milican 9-6-1865
Burk, Susan to Joshua Murphy 8-13-1869 (8-15-1869)
Burkhart, L. E. to James P. Reynolds 8-11-1880
Burnett, Luaner A. to William R. Perry 8-25-1879
Burnett, Mary Frances to William H. Lovlas 9-18-1878 (9-28-1878)
Burton, Nancy Cenith to Alvin Burton 9-21-1880
Burton, Tennessee to John Brunett 11-13-1866
Buttram, Arbanna to James Williby 6-20-1878 (6-21-1878)
Buttram, Catharine to Marion Strunk 9-4-1879
Buttram, Clara Jane to Elswick Thompson 3-20-1868 (3-26-1868)
Buttram, Ellan to M. L. Atkins 2-1-1867
Buttram, Huldy to Calaway Ellis 3-22-1875 (3-28-1875)
Buttram, Lucretia to Joseph Burnett 9-25-1860
Buttram, Lucretia A. to Calvin Chambers 10-19-1876
Buttram, Martha to James Barten 3-22-1879
Buttram, Martha L. to Jacob Thompson 2-23-1873
Buttram, Masha to Richard Pemberton 7-27-1876
Buttram, Millie to A. S. McCarthy 3-26-1877 (3-27-1877)
Buttram, Orbanna to Jordian Buttram 7-29-1854
Buttram, Parazidia to Esau Thompson 1-4-1869 (1-7-1869)
Buttram, Pherbia to Thomas Deboys 12-30-1877
Buttram, Polly to Baty Cecil 11-4-1874 (11-6-1874)
Buttram, Rachel Mira? to William Newport 3-14-1868 (3-19-1868)
Buttram, Rhoda to Julen Potter 8-25-1855 8-26-1855
Buttram, Rosa to Jacob Hammon 10-30-1856
Buttram, Rosa Jane to J. S. Duncan 2-24-1870 3-3-1870

Scott County Brides

Byan, Luisa to Josiah Baird? 3-10-1866 3-15-1866
Byrd, Cristeener to Jerimiah Botts 1-9-1878 (1-10-1878)
Byrd, Elizabeth to Ryer Atkins 10-13-1865 (10-15-1865)
Byrd, Elizabeth to William Hutson 3-26-1872
Byrd, Julia to William Bow 10-14-1879 (10-18-1879)
Byrd, Mary to Riley Chambers 2-17-1867
Byrd, Maryan to Wm. Risden 2-18-1856
Byrd, Nancy to John Epperson 4-24-1870
Byrd, Nancy to Harmon J. Thompson 12-2-1872 12-5-1872
Byrd, Nancy J. to Jacob Neal 2-11-1871 (2-12-1871)
Byrd, Patsy Jane to Henry Low 9-3-1872 9-5-1872
Byrd, Thursy Ann to Thomas Christian 2-1-1872
Byrun, Mary An to Preecher Bird 9-6-1856 9-7-1856
Cain, Permelia to Francis A. Creekmore 1-7-1858
Calhoun, Milly J. to Matthew Mounts 1-14-1878
Cambell, Nancy to David Chitwood 4-2-1860 (4-12-1860)
Canada, Juannah to William Carrol 1-5-1865
Canady, Margerett to Henderson Vanover 9-27-1878
Canady, Molly to John Vanover 11-3-1876
Caroll, Jane to Thomas Morow 10-27-1879
Caroll, Rozanna to C. H. West 10-30-1861 (10-31-1861)
Carrol, Sarah to George W. Lawson 7-8-1864 (7-10-1864)
Carroll, Rozana to Charles H. West 10-30-1861
Carson, Emily Jane to Baty Keeton 10-12-1868
Carson, Jane to William Lay 7-28-1864
Carson, Mary Ann to Tasmon W. Cotton 9-24-1867 9-26-1867
Carson, Polly Ann to Andrew Reed 12-14-1866 12-19-1866
Carson, Sally Ann to Robert Stanley 2-2-1872 (2-8-1872)
Casey, Sarah to John Canor 11-29-1875 (11-30-1875)
Cassifang, Bertha F. to Geo. W. Harrison 9-2-1875 (9-5-1875)
Cecil, Abigail to M. F. Rosser 4-3-1880 (4-8-1880)
Cecil, Artema to Charles West 10-13-1868 (10-15-1868)
Cecil, Emely C. to Pleasant W. Phillipps 2-17-1869 (2-18-1869)
Cecil, F. J. to E. W. Phillipps 9-29-1876 (9-28?-1876)
Cecil, Jane to Emanuel Duncan 3-1-1869 (3-4-1869)
Cecil, Salina to Blagbun L. Phillipps 2-11-1880 (2-15-1880)
Cecil, Susan O. to Newton King 9-13-1866
Chambers, Burnetta J. to William F. Chandler 5-10-1871 (5-11-1871)
Chambers, Charity to W. M. H. Potter 12-31-1873 (1-1-1874)
Chambers, E. J. to Lewis Croly 4-14-1875 (4-15-1875)
Chambers, Elmiriah to Emsley Jeffers 3-31-1855 4-5-1855
Chambers, F. E. to John Thomas 9-23-1880
Chambers, Luanner J. to James A. Smith 3-1-1876 (3-2-1876)
Chambers, Margerett to Emsley Jeffers 10-18-1855
Chambers, Margerett to Albert S. Loyd 10-27-1859
Chambers, Margerett to J. A. Potter 11-15-1876 (11-16-1876)
Chambers, Martha A. to Jobias Risden 1-18-1878 (1-20-1878)
Chambers, Nancy to Claborn Jeffers 5-1-1867 5-2-1867
Chambers, Nancy C. to Winfield Brown 4-9-1872
Chambers, Nancy E. to Julian F. Potter 4-2-1878 (4-4-1878)
Chambers, Pherbia to Berry Bowling 4-5-1878? (4-6-1879)
Chambers, Phoeba to Wesley West 1-18-1870 1-20-1870
Chambers, Polly to Riley Jeffers 12-26-1854 12-28-1854
Chambers, Rebecca to Jacob L. Cross 9-29-1859

Scott County Brides

Chambers, Rosina to Wyatt Atkins 1-20-1871 (1-21-1871)
Chambers, Sarah to Tyrell Hamblin 10-14-1861 (10-15-1861)
Chambers, Sarah to Franklin Jeffers 1-7-1879 (1-10-1879)
Childers, E. to D. C. Small 10-5-1875
Childers, M. Drucilla to James Daughty 4-27-1879
Childers, Nitty J. to Hiram jr. Keeth 8-29-1877 (8-28?-1877)
Childres, Eliza to Andrrew Stephens 5-15-1877
Chitwood, Armelda to David Duncan 6-3-1869 (7-25-1869)
Chitwood, Elizabeth to G. B. Creekmore 7-4-1870 7-17-1870
Chitwood, Elizabeth to David Trammell 12-25-1868
Chitwood, Elizabeth A. to Riley Phillipps 10-5-1867 10-9-1867
Chitwood, Emily to F. M. Chitwood 5-13-1876 (5-18-1876)
Chitwood, Jane to Jonathon Phillips 4-4-1859 (4-8-1859)
Chitwood, Lakey to William Smith 11-17-1876 (11-19-1876)
Chitwood, Lorie to Richard Chitwood 5-17-1876 (5-18-1876)
Chitwood, Lucinda to Wilson Davis 5-29-1856
Chitwood, Lucinda to Ewell Stanley 12-21-1876 (12-28-1876)
Chitwood, Lucy A. to John jr. Carson 1-3-1876 (1-6-1876)
Chitwood, Luretta to Rufus D. Litton 2-1-1869 (2-18-1869)
Chitwood, Marth to Isaac K. Craig 1-16-1861
Chitwood, Mary to Daniel Blevins 8-19-1870 (8-28-1870)
Chitwood, Mary to Robert Simpson 7-23-1869 (7-25-1869)
Chitwood, Nancy to Melton A. Byrd 6-24-1871 (7-1-1871)
Chitwood, Nancy J. to Thomas Barnes 5-27-1869
Chitwood, Polley to Joab Hill 7-23-1865 (7-25-1865)
Chitwood, Polly to A. D. Chitwood 9-28-1869 (10-1-1869)
Chitwood, Polly to Danswell Tramell 10-30-1878 (10-31-1878)
Chitwood, Prissey Ann to Henry Long 10-8-1875 (10-10-1875)
Chitwood, Rachel to Daniel Blankenship 6-8-1877 (6-10-1877)
Chitwood, Sarah to L. D. Chitwood 8-20-1871
Chitwood, Sarah to Isaac Jones 11-24-1865 (11-27-1865)
Chitwood, Sarah Ann to James L. Elswick 2-27-1867 2-28-1867
Clark, Mary E. to James H. Phelps 8-2-1871 (8-20-1871)
Claxton, Bethany to Jonathin Botts 10-2-1877
Claxton, Elizabeth to J. W. Moore 9-1-1880
Claxton, Mary Jane to Jarrett Honeycutt 3-9-1878 (3-10-1878)
Coal, Almeda to Isaac Gadson 3-14-1875
Cobb, Emily to Robert Stanly 3-14-1879 (3-23-1879)
Coffee, M. Jane to James G. Jones 11-17-1866
Coffey, Jane to Harrison Keeton 6-15-1870 6-16-1870
Coffey, Nancy to James Perkins 7-30-1859
Coffey, Nancy to Pleasant Spradling 3-30-1861
Coffey, Rhody to Lewis Perkins 3-21-1861
Coill, Artema to Haron Terry 8-1-1865
Coill, Elizia Jane to Isaac Hill 12-2-1855
Colens, Mattie to Jacob Elder 9-20-1880
Commerce, Susan to Joseph Wallace 7-29-1861 (7-30-1861)
Cook, Cumfet to Peter Bird 4-8-1857
Cook, Druesy to Lemuel Alkins 7-14-1877
Cook, Moumen to Stephen Silcox 3-6-1868 (3-8-1868)
Cooper, E. J. to D. E. A. Strunk 1-9-1875
Cooper, Elizabeth to Reuben Taylor 1-4-1872
Cooper, Ester to Emanuel Cross 4-1-1869 (4-4-1869)
Cooper, Isabella to Lewis Coffey 1-3-1879 (1-30-1879)

Scott County Brides

Cooper, Jane to Abslom Crabtree 5-22-1877
Cordell, Anna B. to R. J. Baker 2-24-1877
Cordell, Elizabeth E. to Rhodes Duncan 11-14-1878
Cordell, Lica to Alvin Stephens 2-20-1862
Cordell, M. E. to Ewell Douglass 2-9-1879
Cordell, Sarah to Granville Stephens 4-12-1856 4-15-1856
Cornillas, Shillotty to Albert Christia 7-18-1875
Cotton, China W. to John M. Cordell 12-25-1860 (1-24-1861)
Cotton, Fanny to Harrison Smith 4-1-1876 (4-5-1876)
Cox, Charlotte to Braxton King 8-23-1880
Cox, Martha to William Riggs 5-2-1875
Cox, Olive to James Cordell 8-27-1857
Crabtree, Betty to Baley Owens 12-4-1855
Crabtree, Mary E. to Riley Smith 12-11-1877
Crabtree, Mary S. to Fredrick Trammell 1-23-1870
Crabtree, Tabbitha to Hesikiah Birchfield 12-7-1878
Craig, Ma A. to J. Q.? Dick 2-16-1874 (2-17-1874)
Creekmor, Helen to Job Meadors 3-3-1856
Creekmore, Mary L. to William Cordell 2-20-1856 2-21-1856
Cross, Catharine to James H. Pemberton 9-28-1867 9-29-1867
Cross, Elizabeth to Harmon Thompson 1-10-1856
Cross, Louisa to Berry Hill 8-23-1877 (8-26-1877)
Cross, Louisa J. to Harmon Thompson 11-22-1873 11-23-1873
Cross, Maria Sintha to J. J. Duncan 8-17-1854
Cross, Mary to Joseph D. W. Sanders 6-1-1880 (6-13-1880)
Cross, Mary J. to George B. Anderson 5-26-1873 8-26-1873
Cross, Nancy to George W. Chambers 3-16-1867
Cross, Rebecca to Granville C. Chambers 4-23-1865 (4-27-1865)
Cross, Rittia to Josiozas? Marcun 9-14-1878 (9-15-1878)
Cross, Rittie A. to Pressly Huckobey 5-29-1878 (5-30-1878)
Cross, Sarah to Ewell Atkins 5-3-1877
Cross, Sarah E. to James jr. Angel 9-8-1879 (9-18-1879)
Cross, Sarah H. to Balam C. Parker 7-5-1873 7-6-1873
Cross, Surreptia to Jacob Roberson 7-11-1855 7-13-1855
Cross, Surreptia to Joel Roberson 9-11-1856 9-13-1856
Cross, Tempy to James Sharp 12-6-1854 12-7-1854
Cruse, Lovina to Carter Hutson 10-7-1874 (10-5?-1874)
Curgis, Bridgett to M. Swiney 3-28-1875
Curtis, Mary to William Hacker 11-17-1859
Dagley, Burtha to James Stanley 12-31-1860 (1-2-1861)
Dagley, Elizabeth to George W. Sharp 9-22-1869 (9-23-1869)
Dagley, Malinda to Ervin Banks 6-28-1875
Dagly, Elizabeth to Hiriam Stephens 4-7-1855 4-8-1855
Daughty, Elizabeth to William Phillipps 3-21-1857 7-25-1857
Daughty, Marylin to David Stanly 11-10-1878 (11-17-1878)
Daughty, Rosa to Josiah Marcum 3-12-1877 (3-15-1877)
Daulton, Frankie to John Johnson 7-23-1867
Davenport, Martha to J. S. Cummins 10-19-1878
Davenport, Martha E. to J. S. Cumins 10-19-1878
David, Emily to Pleasant W. West 9-24-1873
David, Olly to George W. Cecil 8-9-1879 (8-21-1879)
Davis, Anna to Jessie Risden 12-26-1875 (12-25?-1875)
Davis, Armelia to William J. Cordell 2-27-1875
Davis, Ellie V. to Ruford Callist 12-10-1878

Scott County Brides

Davis, Lucretia to Nathan Perry 10-12-1877 (10-18-1877)
Davis, Martha to Jerimiah McCarty 8-18-1876
Davis, Sarah E. to Joseph Richmond 1-23-1880
Davis, Susan to Soloman Stephens 1-8-1876 (1-9-1876)
Debenport, Jane to Pleasant Blevins 11-19-1872 11-20-1872
Decker, Maria B. to William Yowden 8-26-1879
Delk, Maria to Thomas Byrd 2-4-1856
Delk, Parizidia to John Byrd 3-8-1855
Dobbs, Maggie to W. R. Oliver 10-25-1879
Dobbs, Victoria to Adam C. Reed 10-25-1879
Doss, Elvira Evaline to J. L. Litton 1-7-1879 (1-10-1879)
Douglass, Elizabeth to William Tapley 2-28-1867 3-28-1867
Douglass, Emily to W. M. Anderson 10-31-1878
Douglass, Flemon to Elishia Boyatt 11-21-1871 (2-12?-1872)
Dowirs?, Lucinda to Thomas Chambers 7-28-1879
Draughn, Charity to Samuel Smith 5-10-1873 5-12-1873
Drawn, Rutha to John Massingale 1-17-1874 (1-18-1874)
Dugger, Perlina to John Stover 8-13-1870 (8-25-1870)
Duglass, Susanna to Barney Sharp 2-11-1875
Duncan, Burzilia to John Calvin Atkins 3-15-1879 (3-16-1879)
Duncan, Elizabeth to Wright Merony 7-25-1874 (7-26-1874)
Duncan, Elizabeth (Miss) to Andrew Chitwood 10-8-1878 (10-10-1878)
Duncan, Julia A. to Jessie Lay 2-19-1872 (2-22-1872)
Duncan, Louisa Emeline Jane to Champion Duncan 2-2-1860
Duncan, Lucinda to J. S. Acres 2-25-1876 (3-9-1876)
Duncan, Luvania to James P. Walker 6-16-1856
Duncan, Lydia S. to Henry C. Dawn 11-30-1870 (12-1-1870)
Duncan, Martha M. to James Lay 1-24-1878
Duncan, Mary to R. S. Davis 8-8-1874 (8-9-1874)
Duncan, Mary to Jacob Shoopman 5-10-1856 5-11-1856
Duncan, Nancy to Calvin Baker 9-28-1875 (9-29-1875)
Duncan, Nancy to D. E. Low 3-22-1875
Duncan, Parizidia to John C. Atkins 3-5-1879
Duncan, Parizidia to Stephen Jeffers 10-29-1869
Duncan, Rosa to Elishia King 4-14-1860
Duncan, Rutha to Oliver Duncan 3-11-1856 (3-13-1856)
Duncan, Sally to Perleman Ross 8-9-1879 (8-10-1879)
Duncan, Susan to James Parker 6-16-1856 6-27-1856
Duncan, Susana J. to William J. Canada 10-14-1859 (10-16-1859)
Dyer, Mary to John Taylor 3-5-1878 (3-8-1878)
Eads, Sarah J. to Gilbert Marcum 1-20-1871 (1-21-1871)
Edmonson, Sarah J. to Henenson Vaney 10-28-1875 (10-30-1875)
Elliott, Eliza to Hansford Hatfield 4-8-1854 4-9-1854
Elliott, Rebecca E. to Calvin Hugett 1-2-1869 (1-3-1869)
Ellirs, Parizidiar to Alfred Willeby 10-24-1877 (10-25-1877)
Ellis, Arbanna to Joel Buttram 12-26-1866 12-27-1866
Ellis, Clarisa to John Foster 4-1-1868 (4-2-1868)
Ellis, Elizabeth to Reuben West 8-21-1873 8-24-1873
Ellis, Emily to General Phillipps 2-19-1872 (2-22-1872)
Ellis, Lucy to James Foster 2-20-1869 (2-24-1869)
Ellis, Martha Jane to Marion Ellis 8-13-1866
Ellis, Mary Jane to Josiah Marcum 12-24-1869 1-2-1870
Ellis, Rachel to Isaac Reed 1-30-1878 (1-31-1878)
Ellis, Rhoda to J. H. Newport 11-20-1877 (11-23-1877)

Scott County Brides

Ellis, Sarah to James Mattison Elliott 11-15-1860 (11-18-1860)
Ellis, Sarah to Fountain Phillips 7-19-1865 (7-20-1865)
Ellis, Sarah Ann to Willis Ownes 2-29-1872
Ellott, Mahulda to Feril H. Stanly 4-18-1861 (4-21-1861)
Elreath, Seala to Alvin Taylor 9-7-1866
Elson, Virginia E. to Henry Creekmore 9-18-1872 9-29-1872
Emery, Phoeba to Ewell Chitwood 9-20-1868
Emmett, Mary A. to Geog? W. Slaven 8-17-1870
Ervin, Jennie to Dillard James 11-11-1874 B
Evins, Nancy Jane to Wesley H. More 1-28-1866 (1-18?-1866)
Fair, Ellen (Miss) to Ruben M. Denny 11-19-1876
Flynn, Arreny to William Cowen 10-27-1876
Forbis, Relda to Isaac Foster 9-16-1880
Foster, Anna to Elihue McDonald 1-14-1880 (1-15-1880)
Foster, Berthena to William Winchester 2-17-1875
Foster, Elizabeth to Calvin Thomas 2-1-1869 (2-11-1869)
Foster, Emeline to Jacob Ruthford 4-14-1880
Foster, Jane to Marion Duncan 1-14-1868 (1-16-1868)
Foster, Jane to Isaac Wallace 4-19-1870 4-20-1870
Foster, Lewrana to David Troxell 9-1-1869
Foster, Mahulda to J. W. Parsons 4-3-1880 (4-4-1880)
Foster, Marga to George W. Troxell 9-1-1869
Foster, Martha to Hiram Troxwell 3-30-1861
Foster, Martha Ann to John Wesley Worley 11-13-1863
Foster, Mary Angeline to John R. Harness 3-24-1872
Foster, Nancy to John Tralwell? 10-26-1876
Foster, Polley Jane to William Slaven 11-17-1865
Foster, Rachel to Wright Sexton 12-2-1860
Foster, Rhoda Ann to Harmon Smith 4-5-1877
Foster, Sarah to Charles Phillipps 2-11-1868 (2-13-1868)
Foster, Sarah Jane to C. F. Keeton 9-6-1874
Foust, Delitha to S. W. Acres 11-19-1868
Foust, Mary to Eli Sharp 10-19-1869 10-21-1869
Fowce, Nancy Jane to Joseph A. Simpson? 3-5-1866
Fox, Nancy to William Smith 2-5-1860
Frazier, Kate to James M. Omara 5-26-1880 (5-21?-1880)
Fredrick, Delphia to James Cox 1-23-1860
Freeman, Amelia to S. W.? G. Roberds 4-11-1879
Fry, Susana to W. L. Robbins 10-22-1875
Garner, Clartine to Pleasant Mosier 8-31-1856
Garrett, Mary to Pleasant Daughty 8-2-1880 (8-5-1880)
Gentry, Sarah to William Crabtree 9-5-1860
Gibson, Burnettia to W. A. Hatfield 1-6-1866 (1-17-1866)
Gibson, Elizabeth to Marion J. Bruce 5-21-1878
Gibson, M. Jane to John Martin 6-4-1857 6-5-1857
Gibson, Manerva to J. F. Hatfield 5-6-1861 (5-12-1861)
Gibson, Martha to William Perkins 3-9-1876
Gibson, Nannie to Homer Johnson 3-11-1878
Gibson, Sally to Timothy Anderson 7-2-1866
Gibson, Sarah to L. B. Bruce 9-9-1875
Gilbreath, Susan to W. H. Broyles 4-4-1878
Gilbreth, Hanah R. Melda to Manuel Wilson 12-1-1861
Gillas, Anniah? to Thos. H. Johnson 10-24-1870 (11-24-1870)
Goad, Almirah to Daniel Walker 3-12-1866

Scott County Brides

Goad, Arline to Crusoe West 9-11-1877 (9-13-1877)
Goad, Catharine J. (Miss) to George W. Pemberton 7-17-1876 (7-20-1876)
Goad, Elizabeth to John Griffith 11-16-1870 (11-18-1870)
Goad, Elizia Jane to Charley Burchfield 1-29-1879 (1-30-1879)
Goad, Malinda to Andrew Griffith 3-30-1857 4-2-1857
Goad, Mary to James M. Miller 2-1-1864 (2-2-1864)
Goad, Milly to David Brown 3-1-1869 (3-2-1869)
Goad, Nancy Jane to Thomas Sexton 9-24-1866 9-25-1866
Goad, Polly to Micheal Walker 10-6-1877
Goad, Sarah to Andrew Young 9-30-1859 (10-2-1859)
Godsey, Nettie to Macy Robbins 12-25-1879
Goodan, Mary J. to Thomas Hale 7-26-1879 (7-28-1879)
Goodan, Rebecca to John Young 6-27-1856 6-24-1856?
Goodin, Elizabeth to Green B. Camble 4-23-1860
Goodin, Layer? to Martin Goodin 8-8-1879
Goodman, Elizabeth to Joseph Low 9-7-1877 (9--16-1877)
Goodman, Matilda to Alvis Hembree 1-5-1879 (3-20-1879)
Goodman, Nancy A. to Henry Low 12-30-1875
Goodman, Sarah to Jordan Massingale 9-26-1866
Goodman, Sarah J. to Frank Hardy 5-30-1876 (5-3?-1876)
Gosling, Nancy Emeline to John Overton 3-30-1867
Gosnel, Martha to J. N. Clours 8-13-1875 (8-16-1875)
Goswell, Miriah to Ivery F. Griffith 12-15-1876 (12-17-1876)
Grant, Lucinda to E. M. Cross 2-21-1880
Grant, Rhoda to Richard Creekmore 2-17-1877
Gregory, Angelina J. to Joseph Troxwell 12-15-1864
Gregory, Jane to Russle Crabtree 9-15-1877
Griffeth, Esther to Thomas Cooper 5-1-1861
Griffith, Clorie A. to James Drawn 3-29-1877 (4-1-1877)
Griffith, Elizabeth to H. W. Cross 10-16-1871
Griffith, Elizabeth to Riley Sexton 5-6-1875
Griffith, Esther to Robert Price 10-22-1867
Griffith, Franky to E. A. Human 6-8-1873
Griffith, Hatty to Wm. Goad 2-12-1857
Griffith, Jane to Joel Griffith 1-14-1878 (1-16-1878)
Griffith, Malinda to Reddin Lewallen 3-25-1869 (3-29-1869)
Griffith, Malinda to Ingram Phillipps 3-6-1878 (3-10-1878)
Griffith, Mary to Alberson Newport 3-23-1874 (3-2?-1874)
Griffith, Mary to Granville Parker 4-18-1878
Griffith, Rebecca to John C. Henry 9-7-1868 (9-10-1868)
Griffith, Rebecca to Thomas Newport 12-23-1876 (12-28-1876)
Griffith, Rebecca to James H. Pemberton 3-4-1878 (3-7-1878)
Griffith, Rebecca J. to Daniel Acres 11-3-1879 (11-6-1879)
Griffith, Sarah A. to Calvin Robbins 5-20-1875
Griffith, Sophia to Hiriam Sexton 2-26-1858 (3-2-1858)
Grining, Sarah to Pat Gauly 6-8-1876
Hail, Manda J. to George Carson 3-18-1880 (3-21-1880)
Hamby, Elizabeth to William jr. Lay 8-26-1868 (8-30-1868)
Hamby, Rachel to John Roysden 11-29-1866
Hamilton, Sarah (Miss) to George Johnson 7-18-1876
Hammock, Anna to William Thomas 11-3-1860 (11-4-1860)
Hammock, Rutha to Alexander Mills 3-13-1877 (3-4?-1877)
Hammon, Lucinda to G. W. Williams 12-24-1877 (12-25-1877)
Hammons, Lotty to Isaac Gibson 3-16-1866

Scott County Brides

Harmon, Bashaby to David Ryan 9-25-1866
Harness, Delily to C. R. Jeffers 8-18-1877 (8-14?-1877)
Harness, Elizabeth to John Harness 1-5-1860 (2-11-1860)
Harness, Gincy to William R. Harness 8-7-1872 8-8-1872
Harness, Louisa to Jerimiah York 5-18-1861
Harness, Margerett to Micheal Duncan 6-16-1880 (6-26-1880)
Harness, Polly to Henry Duncan 1-5-1860 (1-6-1860)
Harness, Surrelda to John Harness 8-13-1873
Harp, Ella (Miss) to Scott Thompson 3-16-1878 (3-18-1878)
Harriess, Lucrecia to James Jeffers 2-18-1876 (2-20-1876)
Harrison, Nancy Ann to J. W. Jackson 10-9-1866 3-9-1866?
Hart, Reminy to Micheal Costella 6-2-1876
Harwich, Katie to John J. Gillis 4-6-1875
Harwick, Katie to John Gillis 4-6-1875
Hatfield, Catharine to John Honeycutt 10-3-1859 (10-6-1859)
Hatfield, Delitha Lean to Phillipp Davis 2-18-1869
Hatfield, Elizabeth to Henry Cornelas 8-24-1856
Hatfield, Elizabeth to E. B. Keeton 12-9-1866
Hatfield, Elizabeth to Andrew Low 3-20-1870
Hatfield, Elizabeth to James Low 11-22-1879 (11-23-1879)
Hatfield, Kizia to Ewel Keeton 7-23-1859 (7-26-1859)
Hatfield, Kiziar to Reuben Thomas 10-25-1875
Hatfield, Louiza to Daniel Neal 12-24-1867 (12-26-1867)
Hatfield, Nancy E. to Kirby King 9-27-1866
Hays, Nancy E. to David Ryan 8-11-1869
Hays, Polly Ann to Isaac Walker 2-15-1880
Hays, Sarah A. to T. R. Neal 5-9-1878
Helton, Rhoda Ann to William Wilchtree 11-8-1878
Helton, Sarah E. to Joseph Inman 12-10-1876 (12-6?-1876)
Helton, Sarah E. to John W. Stone 2-13-1877
Hembree, Elizabeth to William Lewallen 1-10-1870
Hembree, G. to Phillipp Low 5-7-1866 5-10-1866
Hembree, Rebecca to William Overton 4-24-1876 (4-30-1876)
Hembree, Sarah to Daniel Jeffers 12-24-1860 (12-27-1860)
Herdle, Cora to J. J. Meadors 7-30-1880 (7-23?-1880)
Hicabottum, Elizabeth to Crawford Barnett 5-14-1854
Hickombottom, Abigail to J. W. More 5-17-1877
Hicks, Elizabeth to James S. Lackey 11-3-1873 11-8-1873
Hicks, Frances to Tenton Brown 9-2-1867 9-5-1867
Hicks, Polleyann to Calvin Marcim 3-27-1865 (3-30-1865)
Higgenbotham, Sophia to Noah Strunk 8-8-1870 (8-14-1870)
Hill, E. J. to Nicholas Micheal Sharp 1-7-1879
Hill, Florinda to Moses Stephens 12-27-1860
Hill, Sarah (Miss) to Dock Sanders 9-11-1877 (9-13-1877)
Hix, Emely to Wm. Bowling 3-4-1856
Hix, Salina to John Cox 8-27-1867 9-3-1867
Holdaway, Juliann to David York 11-7-1867
Holeham, Maggie to Jacob A. Booker 8-27-1876
Holess, Millie to James Thompson 7-21-1877
Holt, Almedia to Napolian Moore 8-29-1876 (8-28?-1876)
Holt, Samantha to John Jones 12-10-1874
Honeycutt, Elizabeth to Spencer F. Lay 11-30-1869 12-5-1869
Honeycutt, Louisa to George Claxton 1-2-1878 (1-3-1878)
Honeycutt, Nancy L. to Jonathin Botts 9-11-1874 (9-18-1874)

Scott County Brides

Honeycutt, Rachel to Zachariah Burchfield 3-12-1869 (3-14-1869)
Honeycutt, Sarah to David Trammell 12-4-1865 (12-10-1865)
Honly, Sarah J. to Joshua Stephens 2-1-1872
Hould, Elizabeth to Augusta? Creyson 3-26-1875 (3-28-1875)
Huckoby, Salina to Peter Byrd 3-25-1880 (3-28-1880)
Hudson, Sarah to Doctor Bowling 1-26-1880
Huett, Ferbia to T. J. Loyd 11-20-1867 (11-24-1867)
Huett, Martha A. to Calvin Chamber 10-7-1872 10-8-1872
Huff, Catharine to Geog. W. Meal 9-14-1880 (8?-14-1880)
Hughett, A. E. to L. J. Acres 5-28-1869 (5-30-1869)
Hughett, Lucinda to Robert Sexton 8-26-1871 (8-31-1871)
Hughett, Mandy to Melvin Newport 3-4-1878 (3-7-1878)
Hughett, Mary Ann to Ewell Bowling 2-27-1869 (2-28-1869)
Hughett, Nancy Jane to Hugh Hembree 11-17-1855 11-19-1855
Hughett, Parezidia to Jackson Lay 10-19-1872 10-20-1872
Hughett, Rachel to John W. Newport 1-3-1876 (1-6-1876)
Hughett, Sarah Jane to Luke Bowlin 12-11-1875
Humty?, Luiza to J. W. Smith 8-7-1862
Hurtt, Linda to S. Smith 3-31-1855 4-1-1855
Hurtt, Martha to Eli Gregory 4-13-1879
Hurtt, Martha to Wm. McCoy 11-6-1856 11-7-1856
Hurtt, Scyrene to James Newport 7-6-1867 7-7-1867
Hutson, Elizabeth to E. W. Cooper 1-28-1869
Hutson, Martha A. to Frank A. Perkins 5-9-1878
Hutson, Nancy to Harison Bowlin 12-16-1877
Huttson, Mary to William Byrd 11-7-1870 (11-10-1870)
Ingrum, America to Jessie Gibson 11-30-1875
Jardon, Mary E. to J. R. Smith 10-20-1875 (10-22-1875)
Jasper, Lizzie to Perry Haden 8-19-1880
Jasper, Mahaly to Dan Wheeler 8-19-1880
Jeffers, Arraney to G. W. Penington 10-14-1875
Jeffers, Emely to Jesse York 4-13-1861
Jeffers, Florina to Abslom Cross 9-1-1879
Jeffers, Lucinda to Jackson Thompson 4-26-1856 4-27-1856
Jeffers, Margerett to Feelin Newport 9-19-1859
Jeffers, Martha A. to Newton Duncan 10-6-1870
Jeffers, Martha J. to William R. Byrd 10-15-1879 (10-16-1879)
Jeffers, Mary to Esau Newport 10-19-1874 (10-22-1874)
Jiffer, Laca to Moses Brown 1-6-1864 (1-5?-1864)
Johnson, Elizabeth An to William Brown 12-21-1865
Johnson, Gemima to Thomas E. Meadors 1-16-1858
Johnson, Markett F. to Bardon Young 12-21-1865
Johnson, Milly to G. C. Garlen 3-15-1869
Jones, Elizabeth to Burl Strunk 10-13-1870
Jones, Margerett to Henry Noe 3-9-1880
Jones, Martha to William J. Scott 6-28-1866
Jones, Matty to Sam Wilson 12-24-1877 (12-27-1877)
Jones, Rachel to Willis Wolsey 1-5-1866
Jones, Sarah to Burell King 8-17-1872
Jones, Susan to F. M. King? 10-20-1878
Jourdan, Barbara Ann to Shelby Swain 12-31-1866
Keath, Polly to Hiram Huff 3-13-1877
Keeth, Martha An to Noah Stephens 12-18-1865
Keeth, Mary to Frank Hamby 1-19-1860

Scott County Brides

Keeton, Arbanna to John Hatmaker 1-13-1880
Keeton, Emily to Lacy Atkins 8-24-1875 (8-26-1875)
Keeton, Lita to William Bowling 3-25-1875 (4-5-1875)
Keeton, Mandy to A. C. Dean 11-11-1879 (11-6?-1879)
Keeton, Rebecca to William Rosser 9-21-1871
Kidd, Eliza A. to S. J. Swain 3-18-1877
Kidd, Margerett L. to Ebenezer Litton 12-24-1878 (12-26-1878)
Kidd, Mary to James Lay 10-14-1872
Kidd, Mary E. to Isaac Hill 6-11-1877 (6-13-1877)
Kidd, Susanah (Miss) to J. G. Hatfield 12-18-1877 (12-24-1877)
Kincaid, Tennessee to James Whittenburg 10-2-1879
King, Elizabeth to David King 8-8-1872
King, Elizabeth to Henry B. Strunk 3-14-1867
King, Jane to Thomas M. King 7-20-1880
King, Lensy Ann to G. W. Strunk 7-29-1875
King, Margery to Thomas Angel 4-21-1872
King, Martha to Wesley Buttram 10-25-1870 (1-22-1871)
King, Nancy to J. C. Ross 4-28-1878
King, Omy to Marry King 5-27-1866
King, Polly to William Ross 8-13-1866
King, Rachel to Abner W. Spradling 4-23-1880 (7-23-1880)
King, Rachel to G. J. Strunk 11-25-1875
King, Susa to Joseph M. Stephens 11-29-1877
Kirby, Caroline to Calvin Ervin 12-14-1877 (12-16-1877)
Koger, Relda to Fleoman Dobbs 9-8-1878
Lackey, Sarah E. to Reuben Conatser 11-14-1873 11-15-1873
Ladd, Callie to E. L. Stonecipher 9-2-1875
Lancaster, Missouri E. to Milfred E. Bartley 1-15-1866
Lawson, Adiline to Hamilton Griffeth 9-30-1868 (10-18-1868)
Lawson, Elizabeth to Green A. Blakely 5-1-1872
Lawson, Margerett to John R. Brown 12-26-1866 12-30-1866
Lawson, Nancy to W. R. Chambers 1-13-1866 (1-14-1866)
Lawson, Rebecca to William Miller 11-8-1860
Laxton, Martha to Jeptha Stephens 2-1-1867 2-14-1867
Laxton, Mattie Orlena to Kilonnon? F. Good 1-19-1875 (1-21-1875)
Laxton, Rebecca to C. J. West 12-28-1872 1-2-1873
Lay, Helen to Abraham Murphy 7-19-1879
Lay, Jane A. to Jacob Foster 8-5-1877
Lay, Lucinda to Francis Marion Chambers 9-13-1864 (9-15-1864)
Lay, Mandy to Emanuel Cross 10-24-1868 (10-25-1868)
Lay, Mary to William H. Cross 5-10-1879 (5-25-1879)
Lay, Mary to W. W. Stephens 8-27-1871 8-28-1871
Lay, Nancy to Uriah Murphy 2-6-1872
Lay, Parezidia to John W. Cox 3-11-1873
Lay, Rachel to Squire Freels 12-27-1878 (12-22?-1878)
Lay, Rachel to Henry T. Stephens 8-21-1878 (8-29-1878)
Lay, Rachel D. to T. M. jr. Chambers 1-20-1875 (1-21-1875)
Lay, Sarah to Thomas Chambers 4-29-1863
Lay, Sarah to William H. Hamby 12-16-1871
Leach, Sarah to Wm. Wattson 3-4-1876
Lessler, Sallie to Califer Preins? 12-8-1879
Lewallen, C. J. to William C. Russle 4-3-1875 (4-4-1875)
Lewallen, Clarinday to Thomas Bowling 12-9-1854 12-10-1854
Lewallen, Elizabeth to Elihu McDonald 3-15-1855 7-15-1855

Scott County Brides

Lewallen, Louisa to William Walker 8-19-1871 (8-31-1871)
Lewallen, Lucinda to Nicholas T. Chaney 12-4-1856 12-9-1856
Lewallen, Mary to James Babb 12-11-1868
Lewallen, Mary Ann to Curtis Stonecipher 8-13-1872 8-15-1872
Lewallen, Nancy M. to James S. Stonecipher 9-2-1875 (9-4-1875)
Lewallen, Polly to Calep York 5-7-1866
Lewallen, Roziah to John Mohollon 8-10-1869 (8-12-1869)
Lewallen, Sarah to Berry Bowling 1-28-1868
Lewallen, Sophia to John King 11-28-1876 (10?-1-1876)
Lewis, Mary Jane to James W. Silvers 3-5-1869
Lewis, Sarah to James Vaughlin 4-6-1879
Lewis, Sawannie B. to Milfred Bellew 12-13-1878
Litton, Anna to William Rosser 11-4-1870 (11-10-1870)
Litton, Franky to Ewell Phillipps 7-5-1879
Litton, Lucinda to Joseph Simpson 7-27-1869
Litton, Mandy to David Smith 12-8-1874 (12-12-1874)
Litton, Polly to John Thompson 7-16-1870 7-21-1870
Long, Elizabeth M. to Archibald Allen 5-12-1878
Long, Lucinda to Ewell B. Blankenship 11-28-1877 (12-16-1877)
Long, Mary Jane to Eli Perry 12-9-1874 (12-10-1874)
Lovall, Litha to A. J. Hardick 6-9-1867
Lovett, Louisa (Miss) to Cador Warly 10-3-1878 (10-17-1878)
Lovett, Mary Jane to Elias Worly 3-14-1878
Lovett, Surprony to Elias More 6-23-1856
Low, Elizabeth to Hiram Low 8-24-1874 (8-27-1874)
Low, Elizabeth to William Ward 6-28-1878 (6-29-1878)
Low, Frances to Wm. H. Human 10-3-1871
Low, Jane to Jno. Goodwin 1-30-1859
Low, Louezea to L. L. Atkins 12-22-1855 12-25-1855
Low, Mary to John Massingale 8-21-1878 (8-25-1878)
Low, Myriah J. to Jacob Q.? Cross 1-4-1871 (1-19-1871)
Low, Patsy to John Bunch 4-1-1870 4-4-1870
Low, Rebecca J. to J. H. Hembree 4-1-1874 (4-9-1874)
Low, Ritly Jane to Thomas Atkins 2-9-1857 2-16-1857
Low, Salley to Jordon Massingale 8-17-1878 (8-30-1878)
Low, Sally Ann to Anderson Mason 1-8-1870 1-11-1870
Low, Sarah to Thomas McGee 11-7-1860
Low, Sarah Jane to James Smith 4-15-1880
Low, Serrilda to Jourdan Massingale 1-5-1874 (1-9-1874)
Loyd, Drucilla to John C. Robinson 12-28-1850 1-1-1851
Loyd, Rebecca to Allen Griffith 9-30-1862
Macart, Tempa to Solomon Newport 10-19-1870 (10-20-1870)
Madern, Margarett to Harrison Terrill 8-17-1867 10-16-1867
Mahaly, Rebecca to Elishia Cornelias 12-31-1854
Manning, Polly to William Spradling 7-7-1878
Marcum, Calfernia to David Sexton 8-1-1870 8-8-1870
Marcum, Charity to W. C. Blevins 3-10-1878
Marcum, Felaney? to Green Berry West 11-16-1870 (11-17-1870)
Marcum, Julia Ann to Huston Brown 2-3-1879 (2-6-1879)
Marcum, Lovina to Reuben Cecil 9-26-1874 (9-27-1874)
Marcum, Lurana to Martin Terry? 6-1-1865 (6-3-1865)
Marcum, Luverna to Calvin Gentry 6-5-1862
Marcum, Luverna to Ewell Smith 4-2-1866
Marcum, Martha A. to Trumon Ellis 4-23-1874 (4-26-1874)

Scott County Brides

Marcum, Mary Ann to Wm. H. Logson 7-15-1869
Marcum, Mary J. to Edward Honeycutt 2-16-1873
Marcum, Mary J. to Edward Honeycutt 2-16-1873 2-26-1873
Marcum, Nancy to John Crabtree 5-12-1875 (5-13-1875)
Marcum, Pherbia to Emanuell Phillipps 9-22-1874 (9-21?-1874)
Marcum, Snitha to Zachariah Byrd 4-17-1874
Marcum, Tabbitha to Robert Watson 3-17-1877 (3-27-1877)
Marcum, Winny to John R. Phillipps 12-15-1874 (12-17-1874)
Marcun, Nancy J. to George Eads 6-15-1871
Marcun, Polly Ann to Samuell Burris 12-28-1878 (12-29-1879?)
Mason, Angeline to Huston Caroll 7-30-1869
Mason, Sarah to W. M. Duncan 12-6-1873 (12-7-1873)
Masongale, Julian to Jesse Goodman 4-3-1863 (4-5-1865?)
Massingale, Anna L. to Adam Keeler 12-28-1875 (12-30-1875)
Massingale, Evy Jane to Andrew Goodman 9-18-1877 (9-20-1877)
Massingale, Jane to Jordan J. Keethly 8-30-1870 (9-1-1870)
Massingale, M. J. to Alexander Low 7-17-1869 (7-18-1869)
Massingale, Manervia S.? to Nelson Cecil 9-21-1867 9-22-1867
Massingale, Mary to N. R. Hull 10-2-1876 (10-5-1876)
Massingale, Mary Jane to Michael Law 8-25-1877 (8-26-1877)
Massingale, Pheba to G. W. Grider 7-23-1869 (7-31-1869)
Massingale, Sabry to Milton Shoopman 9-2-1859 (9-15-1859)
Massingale, Salina to John Low 10-1-1866
Massingale, Sousan to John Bruce 6-6-1875 (6-10-1875)
Massingale, Susana to Alexander Caroll 9-25-1872 9-29-1872
Massingale, Tabitha C. to John Reed 5-29-1860 (6-2-1860)
Maxwell, Louisa to Elihue Wilson 10-7-1876
Maxwell, Vina to Willern Willson 10-7-1876
McCally, Louisa to Ewell Lewallen 3-8-1871 (3-9-1871)
McCart, Lyda to Timothy Pemberton 3-10-1873
McClain, Adaline to Alex Russle 7-22-1880 B
McDonald, Almiriah to Willy Carroll 1-10-1870
McDonald, Cristena to Berry Bowling 11-17-1864
McDonald, Dillie to G. W. Strunk 11-18-1875
McDonald, Emily to John Lewallen 12-9-1865
McDonald, Julian to James W. King 8-27-1870 (9-1-1870)
McDonald, Mary Fine? to Abner Phillipps 1-16-1866 (1-17-1866)
McDonald, Millie to B. L. Risden 11-4-1875
McDonald, Nancy to A. S. Lewallen 11-14-1869
McDonald, Parizidia to Scott Keeton 6-21-1876
McDonald, Pharizonia to William Marlow 6-23-1869 (6-24-1869)
McDonald, Sarah to Wm. J. Phillipps 1-1-1876 (1-2-1876)
McDonald, Sarah E. to Geo. W. McDonald 4-28-1879 (4-6?-1879)
McDowell, Ibb. to David O. Conner 8-19-1879 (8-29-1879)
McKiney, Mary Jane to Peter Webster 10-7-1876 (10-8-1876)
McKinley, Jane to Lewis Cameron? 10-19-1878 (10-20-1878)
McPeters, Myriah to Josep Bates 11-22-1856 11-23-1856
Meadors, A.R. to J. L. Gilbreth 12-7-1857 (1-7-1857?)
Meadors, Elizabeth to Granville More 2-14-1859
Meadors, Gemima to Dowswell Tramell 6-14-1866
Meadors, Jane to James C. Ross 2-26-1857
Meadors, Marguett Malinda to Elihu Walker 9-12-1856
Meadors, Nancy to Wm. Angel 8-28-1856
Meadors, Rutha to William Smith 7-19-1874

Scott County Brides

Milican, Seally? to E. M. Slaven 1-25-1866
Miller, Sarah to Steward Slaven 7-27-1872
Miller, Scharlott to James Smith 4-26-1880
Mills, Sarah Jane to Eligiah Perkins 5-21-1863 (5-22-1863)
Minton, Margerett to Wiley Wright 7-22-1880
Minton, Mary Jane to Emberson Strunk 7-7-1859
Moonyham, Catharine to Ervin Miles 10-19-1877 (10-27-1877)
Moor, Lucinda to Mathew Wilson 1-18-1876 (1-19-1876)
More, Mandy to Edward McGerr 5-11-1875
More, Mary An to Mark Sumer 2-25-1860
More, Rebecca to William Willson 2-28-1879
Morgan, Lucinda to Joseph Phillipps 8-22-1876
Morgan, Mary E. to O. R. Bruce 10-31-1875 (11-20-1875)
Morrow, Rebecca to James Wilson 3-20-1870
Mosely, Nancy to William Blagben 12-4-1877 (12-6-1877)
Moser, Sarah E. to A. J. Cordell 2-1-1875
Moses, Malinda to David E. Meadors 7-16-1874
Moses, Mary Jane to Enos King 12-22-1877
Moses, Nancy Ann to John Hinson 8-28-1868
Moses, Sarena C. to Henry Wilson 10-8-1868
Mounts, Nancy C. to William Glover 1-14-1878
Mulnes, Susan to James W. Elam 1-1-1867
Murphy, Margarett Emeline to D. W. S. Tramell 5-8-1869 (5-11-1869)
Muse, Mary Ann to Martin Mellin 12-20-1866
Muse, Pegga to Daniel Penington 7-7-1866 7-10-1866
Neal, Emily to Thomas B. Creekmore 12-5-1876
Neal, Rachel M. to Thomas Hays 3-9-1879
Neal, Sarah A. to James Grant 9-5-1880 (7?-15-1880)
Nelson, Tilda to Allen Hensey 5-10-1876
New, Lutheny to W. R. Vanover 9-11-1874
Newell, Luisa to Jacob Seiler? 8-18-1868
Newels, Martha A. to William Keath 1-27-1865
Newport, Annalisa to C. C. Buttram 2-24-1875 (2-25-1875)
Newport, Eliza to Alfred Brown 3-19-1869
Newport, Elizabeth to Jacob Davidson 3-14-1878
Newport, Elizabeth to H. J. Strunk 1-26-1870 1-27-1870
Newport, Emeline to Marion Sexton 11-18-1868 (11-19-1868)
Newport, Emily to Richard Griffith 6-20-1874 (6-25-1874)
Newport, Julian to William S. Sexton 12-26-1868 (12-27-1868)
Newport, Lucinda to Albert Brown 7-19-1868
Newport, Lucinda to Andrew Griffith 7-3-1865 (7-6-1865)
Newport, Lucinda to Andrew York 3-16-1870
Newport, Lucy Ann to Reddin Birge 5-24-1875
Newport, Mary to F. M. Watters 6-8-1875 (7-20-1875)
Newport, Nancy J. to Thomas L. Phillipps 4-4-1871
Newport, Prissillia to William T. Sexton 3-11-1873 3-13-1873
Newport, Rebecca to Wright Griffith 11-18-1879 (11-21-1879)
Newport, Rebecca to James M. Newport 12-5-1878
Newport, Sarah to Josep Griffith 11-23-1860
Newport, Sarah to Emsley Jeffers 1-5-1875 (1-7-1875)
Newport, Sarah to Jonathin Smith 1-23-1860
Newport, Vicy to John W. Phillipps 4-13-1867
Noe, Lucy Ann to John Wm. Nevels 6-27-1871
Osbern, Barbary to Newton Siler 10-3-1880

Scott County Brides

Overton, Jayne to Stephen Smith 3-2-1865 (3-6-1865)
Overton, Martha to William Overton 7-24-1878 (7-26-1878)
Overton, Mary to John Wilson 8-27-1877 (8-29-1877)
Owens, Margerett to Edward Wilson 4-18-1876 (4-20-1876)
Owens, Rebecca to James Smith 2-3-1863
Ownes, Delila to Julen S. Jeffers 9-2-1880 (9-23-1880)
Ownes, Emily to Calvin Smith 2-28-1874 (3-1-1874)
Ownes, Hiley to Henry Perry 8-29-1876 (8-31-1876)
Ownes, Luvamer Jane to Robert jr. Stanley 1-10-1872 (1-12-1872)
Pambly, Relda to F. M. Debenport 6-10-1871 (6-28-1871)
Parcins, Jane Ann to James Satlaney 6-15-1860
Parker, Clerinda to Winfield S. Phillipps 5-4-1872
Parker, Crelda J. to John M. Phillipps 7-30-1875
Parker, Gilla to John Rosser 10-17-1859 (10-27-1859)
Parker, Lucinda to John jr. Reed 9-4-1879
Parker, Lucindia to William Smither 11-10-1879
Parker, Lucresy to Baley Jr. Buttram 8-16-1855
Parker, Martha M. to Joshua Smith 9-3-1879 (9-4-1879)
Parker, Melvina E. to Eligiah Sexton 1-1-1880 (1-2-1880)
Parker, Nancy M. to Joseph Stonecipher 11-19-1867 (11-7?-1867)
Parker, Relda J. to David Ryan 4-18-1872
Parker, Rosey J. to Andrew J. Ellis 12-17-1879 (12-18-1879)
Parker, Rutha to Jasper N. White 1-29-1880
Parker, Thursy Jane to Martin Ellis 11-7-1868 (11-8-1868)
Parry, Mary to Holbert Childers 6-26-1866
Partin, Eliza Ann to Andrew J. Atkins 1-18-1879
Parton, Rebecca to Wm. Sego 1-7-1858 (1-27-1858)
Patrick, Nancy to Joel Wilder 9-18-1869 9-19-1869
Patterson, Salley to A. J. Cross 1-2-1856 1-3-1856
Peak, Mary to James Griffith 8-15-1878
Peck, Martha F. to J. B. Young 12-10-1879
Pemberton, Jane to George W. Ownes 5-20-1869 (5-23-1869
Pemberton, Parisidia to Elswick Thompson 1-22-1870 1-27-1870
Pemberton, Parley to Wm. H. Carson 5-14-1875
Pemberton, Rosetta to Daniel Griffith 12-16-1873 (12-18-1873)
Pendler, Jerushia Jane to William J. Bowman 9-3-1855
Penington, Delphia to Sterling Sharp 11-27-1876 (11-30-1876)
Penington, M. E. to Lewis Thompson 3-30-1876
Penington, Malinda to Marion Hix 3-6-1865 (3-10-1865)
Penington, Samantha J. to Alvin Laxton 8-26-1870 (8-31-1870)
Penington, Susan J. to W. W. Ownes 7-27-1877 (7-28-1877)
Pennington, Elizabeth (Miss) to James G. Slaven 5-22-1878 (5-23-1878)
Pennington, Lakey Jayne to W. H. Hughett 11-21-1864
Pennington, Manda J. to John Smith 11-7-1870
Perkapile, Villia to Joseph Long 3-27-1875 (3-28-1875)
Perker, Susia J. to Eli Perry 5-1-1879
Perry, Nancy E. to J. S. Neal 3-3-1878
Perry, Nancy Jane to Thomas Taylor 5-26-1879 (5-30-1879)
Perry, Peggy to D. H. Vanover 11-3-1876
Perryman, Minnie to David Brown 5-19-1880
Phellps, Fildiah to Oner Atkins 3-28-1879
Philipps, Melvinia to Claborn Jeffers 6-11-1872 6-20-1872
Phillip, Lucy to William Marcum 4-21-1859 (4-2?-1859)
Phillipp, Emeline to John Foster 9-27-1878 (10-3-1878)

Scott County Brides

Phillipp, Nancy to William R. Ellis 10-10-1876 (10-12-1876)
Phillipp, Nancy to C. C. Sexton 1-17-1868
Phillipp, Peggy Ann to William L. Debty 11-29-1878 (not executed)
Phillipps, Angenetty to Sampson Reed 12-21-1874 (12-31-1874)
Phillipps, Anna M. to John F. Webb 10-11-1874 (10-15-1874)
Phillipps, Arlena to John A. Marcum 1-24-1870 1-27-1870
Phillipps, Creesy to Joseph Guin 9-6-1879 (9-7-1879)
Phillipps, Elizabeth to Thomas Cross 2-14-1878 (2-21-1878)
Phillipps, Emerine to William McBride 11-10-1879
Phillipps, Ester to John Sexton 1-1-1855 1-4-1855
Phillipps, Jane to Pleasant Chambers 12-20-1877 (12-23-1877)
Phillipps, Jane to Oliver Hendree 8-19-1880
Phillipps, Jane to Jasper M. Phillipps 2-4-1874
Phillipps, Jeny to Wm. Cordell 12-29-1869 1-2-1870
Phillipps, Luverna to Dave Acres 9-13-1879 (9-18-1879)
Phillipps, Manda to W. L. Davis 4-3-1869 (4-4-1869)
Phillipps, Mandy to F. M. Brooks 9-15-1874
Phillipps, Margerett to Elswick Griffith 11-11-1879 (11-13-1879)
Phillipps, Martha to Charles West 11-13-1864 (11-20-1864)
Phillipps, Mary to Phoenix Newport 10-10-1876 (10-12-1876)
Phillipps, Mary Ann to Wm. Lawson 9-24-1875 (9-25-1875)
Phillipps, Mary Ann to James Sexton 9-27-1862 (10-2-1862)
Phillipps, Melvina to F. W. Cotton 5-17-1869
Phillipps, Myriah to Maxwell Brown 11-7-1865 (11-10-1865)
Phillipps, Nancy to Reason West 5-7-1857
Phillipps, Nancy E. to James Botts 3-17-1875 (3-21-1875)
Phillipps, Nancy L. to A. J. Thompson 8-24-1865
Phillipps, Pegga to Elswick Phillipps 11-2-1872 11-3-1872
Phillipps, Pernetta to Isaac sr. Jeffers 3-7-1874
Phillipps, Phoeba to James T.? Cecil 1-10-1872 (1-11-1872)
Phillipps, Polly to James Hughett 3-2-1875
Phillipps, Rachel L. to Jacob David 1-15-1876 (1-20-1876)
Phillipps, Salley to Johnathin Slaven 4-14-1856
Phillipps, Sarah to Sampson Reed 5-18-1873 7-1-1873
Phillipps, Sarah to John B. Sexton 3-3-1870
Phillips, Esther to David Hatfield 7-8-1865
Phillips, Esther to David Hatfield 7-8-1865
Phillips, Kizah to David Hatfield 7-8-1865
Phillips, Kizzia Ann to Blagburn Thompson 11-18-1860
Pitman, Sarah to Calvin Chambers 1-26-1876 (1-27-1876)
Potter, Rhoda A. to Alvin Parker 9-7-1870 (9-8-1870)
Powell, Elizabeth to Robert P. Solomon 12-18-1877
Powell, Merions to Joe Johnson 7-14-1879 (7-20-1879) B
Powers, Margerett to Narmis Hensly 9-25-1880
Prator, Eliza Ann to George Bartly 2-4-1867
Price, Elizabeth to James Cooper 2-25-1860 (4-19-1860)
Price, Mary to W. F. Thompson 9-1-1880
Price, Sally to John A. Bales 4-8-1869
Privett, Rosa J. to A. J. Strunk 11-26-1871
Provine, Mary to W. S. Chambers 10-13-1869
Pruett, Mary Jane to Nathan Burton 8-24-1856
Quimby, Missouri A. to George P. Manson 6-27-1875 (7-4-1875)
Ramsey, Martha to Elihue McDonald 4-10-1876
Ramsey, Matilda to James G. Foster 3-5-1860 (3-6-1860)

Scott County Brides

Ray, S. A. to A. S. Killby 1-24-1876 (1-25-1876)
Reatherford, Mary to Calvin Hatfield 4-30-1880 (4-4?-1880)
Redmon, Anna to B. L. Sommers 9-11-1860
Reed, Clerinda to Edward Ellis 12-20-1871
Reed, Darcus to Moses Brown 12-31-1877 (1-3-1878)
Reed, Deliah to W. F. Thomas 3-15-1877
Reed, Eliza Jane to Zekial Newport 8-19-1854 8-17-1854?
Reed, Emily to Samul Carson 11-15-1871 (11-16-1871)
Reed, Margett A. to Charles Collins 12-29-1875
Reed, Martha A. to Jonathin Phillipps 2-3-1869 (2-4-1869)
Reed, Pheobe J. to W. H. Williams 12-25-1879 (12-27-1879)
Reed, Rachel to David Murphy 11-17-1864
Reed, Rebecca to James G. Chitwood 2-16-1865
Reed, Rebecca to Josiah Phillipps 8-1-1870 8-25-1870
Reed, Sally Ann to Thomas Miles 5-29-1879 B
Reed, Sarah to J. T. Smith 3-22-1869 (3-26-1869)
Reed, Sarah to J. T. Smith 3-22-1869 (3-26-1869)
Reliford, Jane to Morris Foster 3-27-1880 (3-28-1880)
Reynals, Mary Jane to Marion Jeffers 3-21-1878
Rich, Sarah Ann to James Griffith 6-2-1871 (6-3-1871)
Richard, Agga to John Smith 2-2-1865
Richardson, Tempa E. to Henry B. Ridenor 1-14-1867
Ridenour, Rosa Jane to Levi Sexton 11-6-1877
Ridner, Milly to Samuell Perry 5-1-1880
Riethley, Pricy to James Hatfield 12-22-1875 (12-23-1875)
Risden, Lurania Rutha to Gideon Duncan 12-21-1859 (12-22-1859)
Robbins, Elizabeth to James L. Phillipps 2-8-1875 (2-11-1875)
Robbins, Mandy to John F. Hughett 3-6-1871 (3-23-1871)
Robbins, Rebecca to John Lewallen 9-4-1877 (9-6-1877)
Robbins, Vicy (Miss) to Jasper Hughett 1-16-1877 (1-18-1877)
Roberson, Elisa to Sanders L. Edward 2-28-1877
Roberson, Sarah to Vilantia Domini 6-5-1879 (6-6-1879) B
Roberson, Sarah Ann to Wm. R. Gibson 3-11-1872
Roberts, Lora E. to Jonathan Smith 9-25-1858 9-30-1858
Roberts, Mary L. to Joel Holt 2-13-1879
Roberts, Mary M. to William H. Gregory 10-22-1879 (10-23-1879)
Robinson, M. E. to Joel R. Hays 8-16-1877
Rookard, Nancy to Hensey T.? Cross 3-6-1876 (3-12-1876)
Rose, Gracie to David B. Cordell 8-31-1856
Rose, Luverna to Milfred Perry 2-29-1876 (3-1-1876)
Rose, Malinda to Hiram Privett 12-25-1866
Ross, Betty Ann to S. B. Durm 6-29-1878
Ross, Catharine E. to William Thomas 9-26-1866
Ross, E. A. to William Cross 7-9-1863
Ross, Kizzia to James Heath 5-13-1878
Ross, Kizziah to Jasper King 5-2-1867
Ross, Manerva to J. G. Stephens 1-26-1856 2-26-1856
Ross, Martha Ann to Joel Duncan 5-1-1880 (5-2-1880)
Ross, Polly to Pleasant King 2-17-1877
Ross, Sarah J. to Edward Smith 10-25-1866
Ross, Weltivia to MSatthew King 6-30-1878
Rosser, Frances to William Honeycutt 12-23-1865 (12-24-1865)
Rosser, Sarah E. to Arther Williamson 5-11-1872
Ryan, Alley to Thomas (or James) Hays 7-3-1856

Scott County Brides

Ryan, Julia Ann to G. B. Davenport 2-3-1879
Ryan, Lurania to John Hays 10-16-1866
Ryan, Mary S. to David Bird 2-26-1872 (2-25?-1872)
Ryan, Polly An to Jacob Litton 7-31-1866 8-2-1866
Saloan?, Emeline to Demsey Golden 7-7-1876
Sandusky, Susan to Josep Cecil 9-20-1865
Sandusky, Tennessee to George A. Bell 11-1-1877
Scarberry, Anna Mallissa to Isaac Wallace 6-1-1880 (6-2-1880)
Scarberry, Lucretia to Willis Springfield 11-19-1880
Scott, Elizabeth to E. R. Duncan 7-7-1857 7-9-1856
Scott, Rhoda to Allen W. Crumley 6-27-1876
Scott, Rhoda A. to J. F. Lewallen 9-20-1871 (9-21-1871)
Sego, Sarah to Calvin Chitwood 10-10-1861
Sellars, A. E. to M. B. Vanover 1-20-1879
Sephens, Jane to Emanuel Phillipps 3-7-1859
Sexton, Catharine to William Griffith 4-9-1866
Sexton, Catharine to William Griffith 4-9-1866 12-9-1866
Sexton, Crisy Ann to William West 9-4-1870 (9-8-1870)
Sexton, Emeline to Samuel Newport 7-2-1873 7-3-1873
Sexton, Emily to John Hamby 3-29-1875 (4-18-1875)
Sexton, Emily to Thomas Walker 1-6-1879 (1-11-1879)
Sexton, Julia A. to William L. Thompson 2-2-1880 (2-5-1880)
Sexton, Julia Ann to Calvin Yancy 8-6-1877 (8-9-1877)
Sexton, Leander to Isham R. Sharp 10-14-1870
Sexton, Leaner to Jerimiah Harness 1-8-1878 (1-24-1878)
Sexton, Mandy to John Scott Phillipps 10-30-1867 (11-3-1867)
Sexton, Mary Ann to Harrison Reed 12-2-1865 (12-3-1865)
Sexton, Nancy to Isaac Taylor 7-4-1880 (7-5-1880)
Sexton, Nancy to General Taylor West 7-20-1866 7-21-1866
Sexton, Oliff to Ruben Hurtt 1-17-1876 (1-20-1876)
Sexton, Orlena to Michel Robbins 10-24-1878 (10-21?-1878)
Sexton, Partily P. to James G. Phillipps 4-3-1876 (4-6-1876)
Sexton, Rachel to Finly Lay 5-19-1877 (5-20-1877)
Sexton, Rebecca Anne to Joel Dyer 3-3-1880 (3-4-1880)
Sexton, Rhoda to William Smith 3-27-1861 (4-7-1861)
Sexton, Rhody A. to William Hamby 10-8-1871
Sexton, Rhoena to Thomas Bigby 1-25-1872 (2-24-1872)
Sexton, Sarah Anne to Jefferson Pemberton 1-8-1863
Sexton, Sarah E. to Alexander Griffith 11-18-1876 (11-19-1876)
Sexton, Tempa J. to John Lay 2-15-1874 (5-17-1874)
Shadoan, nannie to Mark Wilson 8-29-1876
Sharp, Drusey to Calaway Thomas 1-23-1878 (1-24-1878)
Sharp, Eliza B. to Henderson Dobbs 12-15-1878
Sharp, Elizabeth to James M. Newport 1-25-1872 (2-12-1872)
Sharp, Emma to Henry W. Beacham 12-28-1874 (12-31-1874)
Sharp, Florence to Michael Lewallen 12-2-1859 (12-25-1859)
Sharp, Hannah to O. P. Byrd 11-18-1868 (11-22-1868)
Sharp, Helen to S. L. Chambers 3-13-1869 (3-14-1869)
Sharp, Helen m. to Granvill C. Duncan 11-8-1873 10-8-1873?
Sharp, Leodica to John Sharp 2-27-1874 (2-28-1874)
Sharp, Leodicea to Thomas McCoy 7-21-1873
Sharp, Louisa to James Morris 10-26-1872 10-27-1872
Sharp, Martha to David Mixon 8-29-1876 (8-30-1876)
Sharp, Mary A. to John Hoss 10-3-1874 (10-4-1874)

Scott County Brides

Sharp, Mary Martha to Calvin Chambers 6-4-1870 6-5-1870
Sharp, Molly to John Laxton 3-19-1858 3-20-1858
Sharp, Nancy to Luke Anderson 7-20-1877 (7-21-1877)
Sharp, Nancy to W. C. Blevins 8-25-1869 (8-26-1869)
Shelton, Emma to Richard Crabtree 8-28-1878 (8-29-1878)
Shelton, Nancy to Thomas Hicks 4-2-1868
Shelton, Nancy to Thomas Hicks 4-5-1869
Shepherd, Frankie R. to Jobe Perkins 11-29-1877
Shepherd, Jemmima to Willis Worley 2-3-1860 (2-4-1860)
Sheppard, Dusa O. to Charles W. Davis 4-20-1880 (4-18?-1880)
Shoemaker, Clemantine to Ezekial Newport 11-3-1870 (11-6-1870)
Shoemaker, Jane to George W. Stringfield 11-7-1871
Shoemaker, Luesy to Jessie Smither 9-2-1867 9-3-1867
Shoopman, Emely to William O. Hembree 7-23-1859 (7-24-1859)
Shoopman, H. E. to Pleasant C. Blevins 5-10-1870 5-22-1870
Shoopman, Jane to Isaac Risden 1-25-1855
Shoopman, Kiziah to William L. Cross 12-5-1866
Shoopman, Louisa to Jordan Massingale 7-27-1858 (8-7-1858)
Shoopman, Nancy to William Parker 7-3-1872
Shoopman, Sarah to Lemuel Atkins 3-5-1855
Shoopman, Sarah to Richard Pemberton 3-5-1878
Shoopman, Susan to James W. Wright 6-26-1878 (6-27-1878)
Silars, Jenetta to J. M. Cellers 8-30-1878
Silcox, Elizabeth to William Emberson Parker 10-10-1859 (10-13-1859)
Silcox, Martha to Eward Ellis 10-19-1875 (10-31-1875)
Silcox, Phenly to Edward Ellis 7-13-1867
Silcox, Susan to Thomas Lackey 12-12-1859
Siler, Elizabeth to William E. Tramell 1-4-1880
Slaven, Emerine to Martin Penington 3-19-1880 (3-20-1880)
Slaven, Emmarine to G. W. Craft 12-28-1871
Slaven, M. W. to G. W. Smith 9-23-1869
Slaven, Mary A. to Jordon Boyatt 10-26-1870 (11-27-1870)
Slaven, Polly to William Slaven 4-15-1878 (4-17-1878)
Slaven, Rachel to John Slaven 11-19-1875
Slaven, Relda J. to Andrew Slaven 7-8-1874 (7-9-1874)
Slaven, Rutha to Calvin Terry 1-21-1856 1-24-1856
Slavin, Elvis to Ervin Foster 10-18-1864
Smiddy, Isabell M. to W. F. Murphy 5-3-1875 (5-9-1875)
Smith, Ary to Granvill Slaven 9-6-1866
Smith, Charity to Reason Marcum 8-6-1866
Smith, Elizabeth to Daniel Cronin 5-4-1875
Smith, Elizabeth to John Slaven 4-19-1860
Smith, Elizabeth to Sampson Stanfill 5-18-1867 5-19-1867
Smith, Ellen to Kindricke Harmon 9-25-1866 1-6-1867
Smith, Ellen to William T. Penington 6-23-1867
Smith, Emily to J. C. Reed 3-1-1871 (3-2-1871)
Smith, Emily C. to William H. Redmon 11-7-1860 (11-8-1860)
Smith, Etta to William J. Kidd 10-19-1878
Smith, Falby to Ransom Sexton 6-25-1871 (6-28-1871)
Smith, Harriett to Marion Terry 8-19-1865 (8-22-1865)
Smith, Jane to William L. Debty 7-6-1879 (7-7-1879)
Smith, Julian to D. L. Bridges 10-7-1869 (10-8-1869)
Smith, Lidia to Finly Litten 7-31-1876 (8-1-1876)
Smith, Louisa to Jerry Byrd 8-6-1854

Scott County Brides

Smith, Martha to Eligiah Blevins 2-16-1876 (2-17-1876)
Smith, Mary Ann to Jonathin Blevins 4-6-1879
Smith, Mary E. to G. W. Young 10-24-1876 (10-26-1876)
Smith, Mary M. to Hamble A. Ross 9-4-1856
Smith, Matilda to James Davis 4-6-1856
Smith, Nancy to John Marcum 12-22-1861
Smith, Nancy to Ezekial Newport 11-22-1860
Smith, Nancy Jane to Even Creekmore 1-15-1857
Smith, Parizidia to Henry Lay 4-18-1870 4-25-1870
Smith, Polly to Granvill Bradon 1-24-1866 (1-20?-1866)
Smith, Polly to Harmon Burk 4-1-1867 4-4-1867
Smith, R. I. to Stephen Hatfield 2-11-1854 2-12-1854
Smith, Rachel to J. C. B. Tassel? 11-23-1879
Smith, Sarah to William Lewallen 9-18-1877 (9-20-1877)
Smith, Sarah to James Sweet 7-21-1859
Smith, Sarah J. to Melton Goins 2-25-1865 2-26-1865
Smith, Sarah Jane to Melton Gonins? 2-6-1865
Smith, Savanah to A. L. Litton 9-27-1875
Smith, Susanah to James W. Ayers 12-15-1878
Smither, Charlott to Pleasan Jeffers 11-27-1867 (11-28-1867)
Smither, Elizabeth to Samuel Davidson 3-31-1856 4-2-1856
Smither, Elizabeth to John Goad 6-4-1878 (6-6-1878)
Smither, Jennie to Ruben West 7-25-1877 (8-2-1877)
Smither, M. J. to Samuell M. Baker 12-27-1879 (1-4-1880)
Smither, Malinda to J.? M. Risden 9-27-1879 (9-28-1879)
Smither, Malinda to R. C. West 10-31-1874 (11-1-1874)
Smither, Marry to Elishia Bull 9-9-1878 (9-11-1878)
Smither, Nancy to Reason jr. West 11-20-1867 (11-21-1867)
Smither, Patsy Ann to Marion Terry 6-26-1878 (7-7-1878)
Smither, Polly Ann to Phoenix Newport 12-29-1868 (1-3-1869)
Smither, Sarah to Jonathin Lawson 10-16-1876 (10-19-1876)
Smither, Sarah to Martin Parker 6-13-1870
Smithy, Emma to Wm. Robert Lawson 2-27-1879
Sneed, Edy to Jonathan Blevins 4-9-1855
Soloman, Nancy D. to W. H. Sloan 2-13-1877
Soloman, harriett to G. B. Highton 10-13-1880
Solomon, Mary to G. W. Huse 8-28-1877
Spradling, Canzada to Joseph Winchester 6-14-1878
Spradling, Elizabeth to F. M. Miller 4-24-1876 (4-26-1876)
Spradling, Elizabeth to Thomas Stephens 1-11-1860
Spradling, M. J. to Richard Slaven 3-7-1867
Spradling, Malinda to James D. Troxdall 12-23-1863
Spradling, Malinda to James Granville Troxdell 12-23-1863
Spradling, Peggy to James Hunly 1-22-1855
Standly, Parazidia to William Crabtree 3-12-1868
Stanfill, Susana to James C. Blankenship 7-2-1873
Stanfll, Mary Ann to Wm. R. Blankinship 2-11-1870 2-12-1870
Stanley, Emely to Russle Dagley 12-27-1860
Stanley, Rebecca to Winfield S. Chambers 12-16-1879
Stanly, Mary E. to James Crabtree 3-23-1875 (3-24-1875)
Steel, Salina to Jacob Troxell 1-1-1866
Steeley, Mary to Jasper Smith 9-27-1879
Stephens, Anna to Richard Wilson 11-17-1870
Stephens, Elizabeth to Henry Cooper 12-12-1855 1-12-1855?

Scott County Brides

Stephens, Elizabeth to Linsay Cooper 3-11-1861
Stephens, Lenora to Scott Keeton 10-10-1875
Stephens, Lenory to Sterling Chitwood 10-3-1876 (10-5-1876)
Stephens, Martha to Richard Tramell 3-30-1860 (5-31-1860)
Stephens, Mary E. to Martin Kenedy 7-19-1877
Stephens, Mary E. to John H. Williams 2-23-1880
Stephens, Mary L. to James H. Swain 8-24-1879 (8-25-1879)
Stephens, Nancy to Pennedexter Barnett 8-4-1878
Stephens, Nancy to James Slaven 4-2-1857
Stephens, Pegga to Robert Minton 6-2-1858
Stephens, Permelia to Granvill M. Shepherd 12-21-1865
Stephens, Polly to Jackson King 2-11-1869
Stephens, Rachel to James Jones 8-9-1866
Stephens, Samantha J. to Miles C. Murphy 1-19-1871
Stephens, Serrilda to Abriham Leach 6-14-1874 (6-20-1874)
Stephens, Susanah to Anderson Hays 2-13-1875 (2-14-1875)
Stephens, Sylvania to Luke Wadkins 1-15-1875
Stephens, Synthia to Anderson Spradling 9-14-1865
Stidheam, Elizabeth to Richard Hill 4-10-1877 (4-22-1877)
Strunk, Artinisey to G. W. Cellars 10-29-1875
Strunk, Delphia S. to James H. Hill 10-15-1859
Strunk, Delphia S. to Thomas D. Masses 7-18-1877
Strunk, Elisabeth to John Wason 7-17-1879
Strunk, Elizabeth to John Coffey 3-16-1861 (3-17-1861)
Strunk, Ester R. to Joshua Duncan 4-16-1876 (4-21-1876)
Strunk, Helen to James G. Davenport 1-9-1869 (1-7?-1869)
Strunk, Kiziah to Allen McDonald 2-15-1877
Strunk, Lena to Thomas McIntire 7-3-1880
Strunk, Lucinda to Marion Murphy 4-4-1870 4-7-1870
Strunk, Lucy to W. H. Cordell 3-18-1861
Strunk, Marica to R. M. Frosts 8-1-1874
Strunk, Nancy to Isham Jones 7-28-1864
Strunk, Nancy to Nelson Meadors 2-1-1880
Strunk, Nancy to Baly Roberts 3-16-1856
Strunk, Nancy E. S. to Joseph M. Cordell 12-6-1866
Strunk, Polly to Joshua Moses 11-10-1870 (11-24-1870)
Strunk, Rena to Patrick O'Brian 7-25-1875
Strunk, Sarah to F. A. Duncan 1-7-1869
Strunk, Sarah to Thomas Gant 3-22-1876 (3-23-1876)
Strunk, Sarah A. to J. E. Bowling 6-19-1875
Strunk, Sarilda to Reuben Stephens 4-10-1860
Strunk, Silvia to William Buttram 2-14-1872
Strunk, Sylva to Eligiah Terry 7-29-1866
Strunk, Zilpha to Harrison Jones 11-6-1859
Sumner, Caroline to James Henry Sellars 12-6-1867
Surber, Mary C. to W. R. Riley Jasper 3-28-1879
Sweet, Catharine to William R. Risden 8-4-1877 (8-5-1877)
Sweet, Elizabeth to Jessie Hicks 6-21-1876 (6-29-1876)
Sweet, Mary to Isaac Harden 6-13-1868
Sweet, Nancy to John Smith 4-13-1859
Tackett, Sarah to Henry Hill 4-18-1860 (4-19-1860)
Tapley, Olly to Isaac Cecil 12-18-1859
Taylor, Anna to Minza Hamons 7-4-1858
Taylor, Elizabeth to Joel Meadors 12-25-1871

Scott County Brides

Taylor, Ellen to Leroy Wilson 10-10-1878
Taylor, Gemmina J. to Eli Cooper 12-11-1871
Taylor, Louisa C. to James L. Litton 1-3-1876 (1-13-1876)
Taylor, Malinda to James Gibson 9-1-1870
Taylor, Martha to Gideon Strunk 1-2-1862
Taylor, Mary to J. C. Creekmore 7-18-1872 9-29-1872
Taylor, Mary E. to W. A. Smith 4-1-1875
Taylor, Nancy to William Chitwood 2-26-1879 (2-20?-1879)
Taylor, Nancy to David Stephens 8-28-1872
Taylor, Polly to William Childers 8-12-1880
Taylor, R. M. to J. F. Cooper 12-11-1871
Tengel?, Eliza J. to James Harmon 12-27-1868
Terry, Emily (Miss) to John Byrd 3-19-1878 (3-21-1878)
Terry, H. E. to G. W. Litton 9-25-1876 (9-29-1876)
Terry, Ithema to Jesse Risden 10-29-1858 (11-2-1858)
Terry, Lucinda to John, Jr. Carson 9-25-1873
Terry, Lurany to Charles Foster 8-12-1875 (8-15-1875)
Terry, Malinda to Jackson G. Smith 5-19-1860 (5-20-1860)
Terry, Nancy J. to Jackson Carson 10-4-1871
Terry, Sureptia to John Blevins 2-14-1870 2-15-1870
Thomas, Emeline to Isaac Thomas 4-2-1872 (4-4-1872)
Thomas, Emily to George Smith 6-3-1869
Thomas, Martha to Joshua Duncan 1-6-1871 (1-13-1871)
Thomas, Nancy to Hamilton Brown 9-9-1875 (9-12-1875)
Thomas, Rachel to John Parker 7-15-1880
Thomas, Rebecca to Daniel Sexton 4-6-1868 (4-8-1868)
Thomas, Rebecca to Jackson Smith 1-31-1855 2-2-1855
Thomas, loucinda to William R. Cecil 8-4-1873 8-17-1873
Thompson, Eliza Jayne to Sampson Reed 7-13-1864 (7-14-1864)
Thompson, Elizabeth to D. H. Hammock 9-15-1879
Thompson, Kiziah Ann to William jr. Newport 10-10-1867
Thompson, Lucinda to George Webb 3-23-1871 (4-6-1871)
Thompson, Martha to Reuben Smither 4-12-1874
Thompson, Martha Jane to James L. Chitwood 2-28-1878
Thompson, Mary Jane to G. P. Dick 5-3-1880 (5-13-1880)
Thompson, Nancy to Rufus Asberry Hammock 12-27-1879 (1-1-1880)
Thompson, Nancy Clay to Isaac Jeffers 5-18-1874
Thompson, Parrella to Henry C. Massingale 4-11-1878
Thompson, Pernetta Jane to Henderson Blankenship 1-12-1876 (1-15-1876)
Thompson, Pheba Jane to Robert Phillips 3-29-1866
Thompson, Polly to James S. Lockey 9-3-1866 9-4-1866
Thompson, Rachel to W. H. Davis 4-29-1869 (5-2-1869)
Thompson, Rebecca to Hiram Filser 7-14-1876 (7-27-1876)
Thompson, Rebecca J. to John Riley Phillipps 8-29-1871 (8-31-1871)
Thompson, Rhody Ann to James Asher 12-13-1869 12-18-1869
Thompson, Salley to James M. Penington 7-5-1866
Thompson, Sally to James M. Penington 7-5-1866
Thompson, Sarah to John M. Hall 9-9-1876 (9-10-1876)
Thompson, Silvania to L. D. Sharp 9-11-1880 (7?-30-1880)
Todd, Martha J. to L. B. Goad 11-21-1873
Todd, Mary E. to J. R. O. Redman 10-22-1877 (10-20?-1877)
Todd, Missouri to Columbus Parker 7-15-1879 (7-17-1879)
Toole, M. A. to P. B. Dunn 4-24-1876 (4-25-1876)
Tramell, Lucinda to Joseph Stephens 3-26-1866

Scott County Brides

Tramell, Lucinda Jane to Robert Burchfield 12-28-1865
Tramell, Lucinda Jayne to Robert Birchfield 12-25-1865
Tramell, Margerett to A. J. Strunk 5-28-1878 (5-23?-1878)
Tramell, Nancy to Thomas Ross 11-14-1879
Tramell, Valeyor? to Harvy Chitwood 2-25-1874 (3-16-1874)
Trammell, Armeldy to William Baird 6-6-1861
Trammell, Eliza J. to Joseph Siler 4-25-1875 (6-25-1875)
Trammell, Elizabeth to Thomas McIntyre 10-10-1879
Trammell, Elizabeth to Andrew Thompson 3-17-1869 (4-1-1869)
Trammell, Elizijane to William Burton 6-1-1856
Trammell, Emeline to James Blankenship 8-13-1871
Trammell, Gemima to Caswell Blankenship 5-8-1877 (5-13-1877)
Trammell, Lucinda to Wm. H. Long 9-7-1869 (9-9-1869)
Trammell, Mary Jane to Joel C. Chitwood 3-22-1876 (3-23-1876)
Trammell, Melvina to William A. Crabtree 10-24-1874 (10-25-1874)
Trammell, Nancy to Rhodes Stanley 5-19-1872
Trammell, R. J. to Whiticar Phillipps 12-28-1874
Trammell, Salley to James Anderson 12-23-1855
Trammell, Sarah to Joshua Duncan 10-5-1877
Trammell, Tabbitha to Jesse Daughty 11-1-1855
Troxel, Martha to Joseph Troxel 6-22-1866
Troxwell, Jane to Isaac Foster 1-15-1870
Troxwell, Relda to Tolbert Roberts 9-31-1880 (10-30-1880)
Troxwell, Tabbitha to Archibald Roach 10-30-1880
Turner, M. A. to Wm. Morris 5-3-1876
Upchurch, Rebecca J. to Hiram M. Wattson 6-24-1872
Valentine, Sarah to John McCarty 3-9-1875
Vanover, Catharine to Critenden Stephens 3-26-1877 (3?-1-1877)
Vanover, Dorcas to William H. Murphy 3-14-1861
Vanover, Eliza to Samuel Vanover 9-25-1867
Vanover, M. A. to William Taylor 8-11-1877
Vanover, Mary to James Stephens 12-25-1876 (12-23?-1876)
Vanover, Sarah to T. C. Perry 5-10-1877
Vanover, Sarrah to David Perry 4-4-1855
Vincens, Ratty to W. M. Stepp 12-29-1875 (1-2-1876)
Walden, Mary E. to C. C. Newport 5-17-1878 (5-18-1878)
Walker, Betty Ann to W. S. Willson 3-16-1876
Walker, Seney Ann to David Anderson 10-23-1879
Walkerson, Bell to Lawrence Brown 9-25-1881
Wallen, Margarett E. to D. A. Gregory 8-28-1872
Wallice, Visa to Isaac Reed 9-15-1873 9-18-1873
Ward, Allis to William Lowery 4-20-1878
Wasson, Elizabeth to G. W. Lovett 7-4-1878
Watters, Jane to Harden Coffey 7-31-1866
Watters, Louisa to Major Reynolds 10-25-1860
Wattson, Rebecca Jane to Abslom T. Boyatt 2-28-1879
Webb, Emiline (Miss) to Jefferson Cummings Pemberton 12-29-1877 (1-2-1878)
Webb, Jane to Marion Davis 1-28-1879
Webb, Nancy to Jno. Eadds 1-20-1871 (1-21-1871)
Webb, Rebecca to Alexander S. Alley 9-23-1854
Welch, Molly M. C. to J. R. Freeman 11-7-1875 (11-8-1875)
West, Catharine to Doswell Stephens 11-7-1869
West, Lucinda to Richard Stringfield 12-27-1864
West, Martha to John Daughty 8-19-1878 (8-20-1878)

Scott County Brides

West, Nancy to Andrew Thomas 10-16-1879
West, Parizidia to Geog. Washington Thompson 2-3-1879 (3-6-1879)
West, Polly to Daniel Chambers 12-13-1874
West, Sarah to William jr. Smith 9-17-1876 (9-23-1876)
White, Elizabeth R. to George Troxwell 11-27-1865
White, Lizzie to Toney Jones 2-24-1880 (2-26-1880) B
White, Lucinda R. to G. W. Kidd 5-8-1876
Whiting, Sarah to Jerry Clark 12-18-1875
Wilhite, Elender Jane to S. L. Babb 4-21-1877 (4-22-1877)
Wilhite, Sarah to David Babb 3-8-1878 (3-10-1878)
Willhite, Rebecca to Jerrymiah Chambers 2-4-1855 2-27-1855
Willhite, Sarah to Samuel Carson 10-28-1867 (10-31-1867)
Williams, Dolly to Sirens Rast 5-7-1854
Williams, Frances to George F. Brown 1-26-1880
Williams, Martha to Ewell Cross 1-12-1874
Williams, Mary Jane to Stephen E. Davis 1-11-1868
Williams, Nancy Ann to Robert Miller 1-11-1879 (1-12-1879)
Williams, Sarah L. to William Todd 6-23-1874
Williby, Jane to Joseph Bull 6-3-1878
Willson, Martha J. to James Worll? 4-15-1880
Wilouby, Mary to Louis C. Evins 11-21-1879 (11-22-1879)
Wilson, Elizabeth to John Cooper 4-7-1876 (4-9-1876)
Wilson, Elizabeth to John Nathan 11-3-1872
Wilson, Emily to Murry Strunk 1-6-1870
Wilson, L. E. to Jessie Smither 8-7-1878 (8-18-1878)
Wilson, M. E. to Marion Stephens 3-10-1877
Wilson, Mahala to John Rice 11-11-1864
Wilson, Malinda to Jerimier Sumner 7-20-1854
Wilson, Margerett to Benjamin Wolsey 10-22-1860
Wilson, Mary C. R. E. to Franklin Overton 3-10-1879 (3-13-1879)
Wilson, Mary J. to John Wilson 10-2-1873
Wilson, Nancy J. to Alexander Wilson 10-28-1874
Wilson, Nancy J. to Alexander Wilson 10-28-1874
Wilson, Rebecca E. to Franklin Overton 10-11-1867 (10-12-1867)
Wilson, Susan to John Shepherd 5-29-1870 5-30-1870
Wimberley, Mattie to James F. Smith 3-3-1881
Winchester, N. E. to Isam Spradling 8-18-1876
Winchester, Polly to Alvin Wattson 9-12-1878
Winchester, Sarah to David Boyatt 4-27-1867
Winchester, Susan to William Spradling 4-27-1867
Wirt, Mahala to Peter Mayfield 8-4-1860
Wood, Sarah J. to Reuben Meadors 12-2-1874 (12-27-1874)
Wootson, Sarah to Jessie Gibson 6-15-1872 6-19-1872
Worly, Martha to Elias Lovett 12-20-1878
Yancy, Elizabeth to Huston Jeffers 4-30-1872
Yancy, Phoeba J. to David Jeffers 1-27-1871 (2-2-1871)
York, Lucinda to Oliver Jeffers 6-17-1867
York, Malinda to Champion Jeffers 5-17-1866
Young, Anira C. to Samuell A. Lewallen 9-6-1879 (9-9-1879)
Young, Elizabeth to Joseph Davis 11-17-1865 (12-5-1865)
Young, Elizabeth to Thomas Moffit 3-19-1879 (3-23-1879)
Young, Elizabeth to Thomas Moffit 3-19-1879 (3-28-1879)
Young, Lizzie C. to Nathaniel G. McCoy 3-12-1878 (3-13-1878)
Young, Lucy to W. D. Webb 3-27-1876 (3-30-1876)

Scott County Brides

Young, Maledun? to Cambell Lewallen 10-12-1865
Young, Martha to John Diden 9-11-1872 9-12-1872
Young, Mary to Ali Smith 3-3-1880
Young, Purdyan to James Goad 3-31-1855
Young, Rozana to Reuben Griffith 4-4-1874 (4-9-1874)
Young, Vetha Frances to Lenord Peak 8-10-1877 (8-11-1877)
_____, (bride omitted) to Ely Hill 9-11-1859
_____, (bride omitted) to John O. Massengale 1-29-1863
_____, Melvina to James S. Coffey 11-16-1878